Cambridge Elements

Elements in Middle East Politics
edited by
David B. Roberts
King's College London
Louise Fawcett
University of Oxford
Mohammed Abdel-Haq
King's College London

NARRATIVES OF SINO-MIDDLE EASTERN FUTURES

In the Eye of the Beholder

Mohammed Alsudairi
Australian National University
Andrea Ghiselli
University of Exeter

CAMBRIDGE UNIVERSITY PRESS

Shaftesbury Road, Cambridge CB2 8EA, United Kingdom

One Liberty Plaza, 20th Floor, New York, NY 10006, USA

477 Williamstown Road, Port Melbourne, VIC 3207, Australia

314–321, 3rd Floor, Plot 3, Splendor Forum, Jasola District Centre, New Delhi – 110025, India

103 Penang Road, #05-06/07, Visioncrest Commercial, Singapore 238467

Cambridge University Press is part of Cambridge University Press & Assessment, a department of the University of Cambridge.

We share the University's mission to contribute to society through the pursuit of education, learning and research at the highest international levels of excellence.

www.cambridge.org
Information on this title: www.cambridge.org/9781009297868

DOI: 10.1017/9781009297851

© Mohammed Alsudairi and Andrea Ghiselli 2025

This publication is in copyright. Subject to statutory exception and to the provisions of relevant collective licensing agreements, with the exception of the Creative Commons version the link for which is provided below, no reproduction of any part may take place without the written permission of Cambridge University Press & Assessment.

An online version of this work is published at doi.org/10.1017/9781009297851 under a Creative Commons Open Access license CC-BY-NC 4.0 which permits re-use, distribution and reproduction in any medium for non-commercial purposes providing appropriate credit to the original work is given and any changes made are indicated. To view a copy of this license visit https://creativecommons.org/licenses/by-nc/4.0

When citing this work, please include a reference to the DOI 10.1017/9781009297851

First published 2025

A catalogue record for this publication is available from the British Library

ISBN 978-1-009-53920-3 Hardback
ISBN 978-1-009-29786-8 Paperback
ISSN 2754-7817 (online)
ISSN 2754-7809 (print)

Cambridge University Press & Assessment has no responsibility for the persistence or accuracy of URLs for external or third-party internet websites referred to in this publication and does not guarantee that any content on such websites is, or will remain, accurate or appropriate.

For EU product safety concerns, contact us at Calle de José Abascal, 56, 1°, 28003 Madrid, Spain, or email eugpsr@cambridge.org

Narratives of Sino-Middle Eastern Futures

In the Eye of the Beholder

Elements in Middle East Politics

DOI: 10.1017/9781009297851
First published online: August 2025

Mohammed Alsudairi
Australian National University

Andrea Ghiselli
University of Exeter

Author for correspondence: Mohammed Alsudairi,
Mohammed.Alsudairi@anu.edu.au

Abstract: *Narratives of Sino-Middle Eastern Futures* attempts to discern the future trajectory and endpoint of Sino-Middle Eastern relations – are we on the precipice of a post-American Chinese hegemony in the region? Or are we reaching the outer limits of what is feasible within what are essentially transactional ties? Drawing on a wide range of multilingual sources from 2010 to 2023, and based on a framework of thin constructivism, the Element delves into Saudi, Syrian, and Chinese elite narratives regarding the Middle Eastern regional order and China's envisaged place within it. By centring local perspectives, it offers insights into how these actors – with diverse positionalities in the region (vis-à-vis the United States) and different national capabilities – are debating the future of China in the Middle East, and what the juxtaposition of their multiple narratives mean for where things are headed. This title is also available as Open Access on Cambridge Core.

Keywords: China, Middle East, Regional Order, Great Power Transitions, Narratives

© Mohammed Alsudairi and Andrea Ghiselli 2025

ISBNs: 9781009539203 (HB), 9781009297868 (PB), 9781009297851 (OC)
ISSNs: 2754-7817 (online), 2754-7809 (print)

Contents

Introduction   1

China: Adjusting to a Changing Regional Order   18

Saudi Arabia: Forging a New Regional Order   34

Assadist Syria: Waiting for a New Regional Order   51

Conclusion   65

Introduction

The post-American era in the Middle East arguably began in the early 2010s as elites in the United States (US), compelled by the strategic imperative of pivoting to the Asia-Pacific to deal with an ascendant People's Republic of China (PRC), downgraded the region's strategic importance.[1] The convulsion of Arab states with popular uprisings and the tepid support from the US for its long-standing allies in Bahrain and Mubarakian Egypt, in conjunction with the dramatic policy shifts across the Obama and Trump administrations over the Islamic Republic of Iran and Assadist Syria, gave weight to the perception among regional stakeholders (and outside observers) that an epochal shift was underway.[2] Local state actors, ranging from Türkiye to the disparate member-states of the Gulf Cooperation Council (GCC), responded to this development by coalescing into ever-shifting alignments espousing different ideo-political visions and agendas.[3] This competition was amplified further by the power vacuums – and, consequently, threats and opportunities – that had materialised in many divided and weakened polities in the Arab world, such as Iraq, Syria, Yemen, Libya, and Sudan.[4] The Middle East regional order thus entered the 2020s in a state of fluid transition evocative of Antonio Gramsci's description of his own era: 'the old [authority] is dying and the new cannot be born; in this interregnum a great variety of morbid symptoms appear'.[5]

Amidst this turbulence, local state actors endeavoured to build new relationships with a variety of non-US external powers. Over the years, the PRC has emerged as one of the most important in this regard, driven in large part by its voracious appetite for energy. In 1993, it became a net importer of hydrocarbons and since 2017 has assumed the status of the world's largest importer by volume, with the region being the source of nearly half of its imports.[6] Its companies have aggressively expanded their presence in Middle Eastern markets,

---

[1] Hillary Clinton, 'America's Pacific Century', *Foreign Policy*, 11 October 2011, https://foreignpolicy.com/2011/10/11/americas-pacific-century/; Fawaz A. Gerges, 'The Obama Approach to the Middle East: The End of America's Moment?', *International Affairs* 89, no. 2 (March 2013): 299–323.

[2] For a discussion on how the US has changed the Middle Eastern regional order, see Waleed Hazbun, 'In America's Wake: Turbulence and Insecurity in the Middle East', in March Lynch and Amaney Jamal (eds.), *Shifting Global Politics and the Middle East, POMEPS Studies* 34 (POMEPS, 2019), 14–17.

[3] Mehran Kamrava, 'Hierarchy and Instability in the Middle East Regional Order', *International Studies Journal* 14, no. 4 (2018): 1–35.

[4] Michael Hudson (ed.), *The Crisis of the Arab State* (Belfer Center, 2015), 10–11.

[5] Antonio Gramsci, *The Prison Notebooks* (International Publishers, 1971), 275.

[6] 'How Is China's Energy Footprint Changing?' *ChinaPower*, undated, https://chinapower.csis.org/energy-footprint/.

as shown by the constant rise in the value of their investment, exports, and contracts for new infrastructure projects.[7] The Belt and Road Initiative (BRI), launched in 2013, added further momentum to these economic entanglements, with nearly all regional states, with the exception of Israel, joining it.[8] In conjunction, the number of 'strategic partnerships' (*Zhànlüè huŏbàn guānxi*), comprehensive or otherwise, has gradually expanded to include all the key regional players, reflecting the growing robustness of Sino-Middle Eastern ties in policy areas beyond the purely economic.[9] More cautiously, the PRC has also waded into regional conflicts through special envoys and ad hoc mediation efforts,[10] as well as at the United Nations Security Council (UNSC), where its vetoes on resolutions targeting Assadist Syria have been most felt.[11] Militarily, the region hosts the PRC's first military base overseas, established in Djibouti in 2017, and Chinese warships have been active in anti-piracy missions in the Gulf of Aden since 2008.

Though the Middle East has never been identified by Chinese policymakers and researchers as a core area of PRC strategic interest,[12] it has nevertheless attained – as indicated by many of these developments – greater importance over the years: this is evidenced by the issuance of white papers and roadmaps calling for the cultivation of deeper relations, including the *Arab Policy Paper* (2016), the *China-Arab States Forum Action Plan* (2020), and the PRC Foreign Ministry's *Report on Sino-Arab Cooperation in the New Era* (2022).[13] President Xi Jinping's two high-profile state visits to the

---

[7] For data on the PRC's economic presence in the Middle East, see ChinaMed, www.chinamed.it/chinamed-data/middle-east; on its diasporic and cultural presence, see Yuting Wang, *Chinese in Dubai: Money, Pride, and Soul-Searching* (Brill, 2020); On its security linkages there, see Andrea Ghiselli, *Protecting China's Interests Overseas: Securitization and Foreign Policy* (Oxford University Press, 2021) and Philip Potter and Chen Wang, *Zero Tolerance: Repression and Political Violence on China's New Silk Road* (Cambridge University Press, 2022).

[8] 'Profiles', *Belt and Road Portal*, undated, https://eng.yidaiyilu.gov.cn/list/c/10076.

[9] Jonathan Fulton, 'Weekend Essay: China's Partnership Diplomacy in the Middle East', *The China-MENA Newsletter*, 15 June 2024, https://chinamenanewsletter.substack.com/p/weekend-essay-chinas-partnership.

[10] China has had a special envoy for the Middle East since 2002 and one dedicated to the conflict in Syria since 2016. Its mediation – beyond the brokerage of the well-known Saudi–Iranian détente – also includes that between the US and the Islamic Republic over nuclear proliferation; see John Garver, 'China–Iran Relations: Cautious Friendship with America's Nemesis', *China Report* 49, no. 1 (2013): 69–88.

[11] Courtney Fung, *China and Intervention at the UN Security Council* (Oxford University Press, 2019).

[12] Chuchu Zhang, 'Bridging the Gap between Overseas and Chinese Perceptions on Sino-Middle Eastern Relations: A Chinese Perspective', *Globalizations* 18, no. 2 (2021): 273–284.

[13] The State Council of the People's Republic of China, 'Zhongguo dui alabo guojia zhengce wenjian (quanwen)' ('Full text of China's Arab Policy Paper'), January 2016, www.gov.cn/xinwen/2016-01/13/content_5032647.htm; Ministry of Foreign Affairs of the

Middle East, the first (2016) marked by an address to the Arab League in Cairo, and the second (2022) crowned with a major Sino-Arab summit in Riyadh, testify further to this newfound significance.[14] The discernible shifts in region-wide interactions with respect to issues of core interest to the PRC – for instance, the contrasting reactions of states to the 2009 Urumchi riots and the post-2017 Xinjiang repressive campaigns – is suggestive of the Middle East's growing relevance to Chinese diplomacy in its confrontation with the 'West'.[15]

When situated alongside perceptions of American decline in the Middle East, the PRC's expanding footprint has unsurprisingly generated much in the way of debate concerning whether it will be the harbinger of a new regional order or not.[16] Intensifying Sino-American rivalry, depicted as global and all-encompassing in scope, informs many of these assessments.[17] One need only take a cursory look at how Chinese-linked infrastructures, technologies, and even diplomatic initiatives in the region

---

People's Republic of China, 'Zhongguo shi zhongdong guojia changqi kekao de zhanlve huoban' ('China is a reliable strategic partner for the Middle East'), 30 March 2021, https://shorturl.at/YdXnw; China–Arab States Cooperation Forum, 'Zhongguo – Alabo guojia hezuo luntan 2020 nian zhi 2022 nian xingdong zhixing jihua' ('China–Arab States Cooperation Forum Action Plan for 2020–2022'), 10 August 2020, www.chinaarabcf.org/lthyjwx/bzjhywj/djjbzjhy/202008/t20200810_6836922.htm; Ministry of Foreign Affairs of the People's Republic of China, 'Xinshidai de zhonga hezuo baogao' ('Report on China–Arab Cooperation in the New Era'), 1 December 2022, www.fmprc.gov.cn/zyxw/202212/t20221201_10983991.shtml.

[14] 'Xi Jinping zai alabo guojia lianmeng zongbu de jiangyan (quanwen)' ('Xi Jinping's speech at the Arab League Headquarters (full text)'), *Xinhua*, 22 January 2016, www.xinhuanet.com//world/2016-01/22/c_1117855467.htm; 'Xi Jinping zai shoujie zhongguo-alabo guojia fenghui kaimushi shang de zhuzhi jianghua' ('Xi Jinping's keynote speech at the opening ceremony of the First China–Arab States Summit'), *Xinhua*, 9 December 2022, www.news.cn/world/2022-12/10/c_1129197334.htm.

[15] Robert R. Bianchi, 'Perception of the 2009 Ürümqi Conflict across the Islamic World', in Niv Horesh (ed.), *Toward Well-Oiled Relations?: China's Presence in the Middle East Following the Arab Spring* (Palgrave Macmillan, 2016), 48–68; Barbara Kelemen and Richard Q. Turcsányi, 'It's the Politics, Stupid: China's Relations with Muslim Countries on the Background of Xinjiang Crackdown', *Asian Ethnicity* 21, no. 2 (2020): 223–243.

[16] For a snippet of the Anglophone debate, see Ariane Tabatabai and Dina Esfandiary, *Triple-Axis: Iran's Relations with Russia and China* (Bloomsbury Publishing, 2018); Camille Lons, Jonathan Fulton, Sun Degang, and Naser Al-Tamimi, *China's Great Game in the Middle East* (European Council on Foreign Relations, October 2019); Jonathan Fulton (ed.), *Routledge Handbook on China–Middle East Relations* (Routledge, 2022); Dawn C. Murphy, *China's Rise in the Global South: The Middle East, Africa, and Beijing's Alternative World Order* (Stanford University Press, 2022). For a contrarian view on American weakening in the region, see Christopher K. Colley, 'A Post-American Middle East? US Realities vs. Chinese and Russian Alternatives', *Middle East Policy*, 27 March 2023.

[17] On the factors, tensions, and continuities the shape Sino-US relations in the Middle East, see Andrea Ghiselli, 'China and the United States in the Middle East: Policy Continuity Amid Changing Competition', Middle East Institute, 9 January 2023, https://shorturl.at/UWaoF.

have been discussed in recent years to discern the pervasiveness of this framing.[18] Even when it is not considered as competing outright with American national interests, the PRC is nevertheless conceived as seeking to detach or draw out the Middle East from the US orbit.[19]

We can thus see two parallel stories unfolding over the past decade – one of American decline (or regional post-American multipolarisation), the other of Chinese 'expansion' in the region – which, when taken together, raise a number of questions that lie at the very heart of this Element: what exactly is the nature of the PRC's relationship with the Middle East? Is it a continuation of well-established patterns of interaction that are essentially transactional in character, or are there nascent signs foreshadowing greater receptivity and willingness by the PRC to play a security-provider role akin to that of the US in the future? Put differently, does the 2010s signify the dawn of a *Pax Sinica* in the region, or a false and illusory start that points to other processes and dynamics there?

To answer these questions, we combine insights from the constructivist, foreign policy analysis and neo-institutionalist literatures to excavate and compare narratives, understood as discourse 'with a clear sequential order that connect events in a meaningful way … thus offer[ing] insights about the world and/or people's experiences of it' and as produced by the foreign policy elites of three states: the PRC, Saudi Arabia, and Assadist Syria.[20] The narratives we are interested in are those that circulated from 2010 to 2023, and mainly those surrounding the problems afflicting the Middle East regional order, on the one hand, and China's potential role within it, on the other. In the following four sub-sections, we provide an explanation of what we mean by foreign policy elites and the significance of their narratives for this study, justifications for our case selections and their relevance to understanding Sino-Middle Eastern relations, an overview of the sources used, and, finally, a roadmap of the sections of this Element.

---

[18] For examples on more recent developments, see Peter Baker, 'Chinese-Brokered Deal Upends Mideast Diplomacy and Challenges U.S.', *New York Times*, 11 March 2023, www.nytimes.com/2023/03/11/us/politics/saudi-arabia-iran-china-biden.html; Maria Fantappie and Vali Nasr, 'A New Order in the Middle East? Iran and Saudi Arabia's Rapprochement Could Transform the Region', *Foreign Affairs*, 22 March 2023, www.foreignaffairs.com/china/iran-saudi-arabia-middle-east-relations.

[19] Jon B. Alterman, 'The Middle East's View of the "China Model"', Centre for Strategic and International Studies, September 2024, www.csis.org/analysis/middle-easts-view-china-model.

[20] Lewis P. Hinchman and Sandra K. Hinchman, *Memory, Identity and Community: The Idea of Narrative in the Human Sciences* (SUNY Press, 2001), xvi.

On Narratives and Possible Futures

In *The American People and Foreign Policy*, Gabriel Almond identified four types of groups that make up the foreign policy elites of a state: the political elites (elected leaders); the administrative or bureaucratic elites (the professional corps of the executive establishment); the interest elites (the representatives of private and policy-oriented organisations); and, finally, the communication elites (academic experts and journalists).[21] Together, these groups generate a discursive field that provides an explanatory coherence to a state's foreign policy choices and actions – something approaching a shared worldview and common vocabulary.[22] For our purposes in this Element, we tweak these categories and focus on the narratives produced by the political (autocratic leaders), the bureaucratic (the cadres and officials of the diplomatic corps), and the communication elites (scholars and journalists). The former two's role in conveying state priorities and stances is clear, but the latter necessitates some clarification with respect to their relevance and ability to reproduce the inner logic of foreign policymaking in the three countries selected: the PRC, Saudi Arabia, and Assadist Syria.

International relations experts, especially in the PRC, are treated in some strands of scholarship as mirrors reflecting their country's foreign policy conventions and preferences.[23] This assumption is mostly based upon how authoritarian environments like that of China structure the discursive output of this segment of the elites: seeking funding, access, and prestige, experts (often embedded within state-controlled institutions) publish opinions and submit policy proposals that are aligned with the perceived preferences of the executive; if they do seek to challenge current choices, they do so in a manner consistent with national interests and the official line, at least from a rhetorical perspective.[24]

---

[21] Gabriel A. Almond, *The American People and Foreign Policy* (Greenwood Press, 1977).

[22] The notion of a discursive field is taken from Michel Foucault, *The Archeology of Knowledge and the Discourse on Language* (Pantheon Books, 1972). On the unique terrain of meanings generated by officialdom on issues of foreign policy (in the PRC), see https://decodingchina.eu.

[23] For representative examples of this approach, see Joseph Fewsmith and Stanely Rosen, 'The Domestic Context of Chinese Foreign Policy: Does "Public Opinion" Matter?', in David M. Lampton (ed.), *The Making of Chinese Foreign and Security Policy in the Era of Reform, 1978–2000* (Stanford University Press, 2001), 151–187; Kai He and Huiyun Feng, 'Why Do Chinese Scholars Matter?', in Huiyun Feng, Kai He, and Xuetong Yan (eds.), *Chinese Scholars and Foreign Policy: Debating International Relations* (Routledge, 2019), 3–20.

[24] Quansheng Zhao, 'Policy-Making Processes of Chinese Foreign Policy: The Role of Policy Communities and Think Tanks', in Shaun Breslin (ed.), *A Handbook of China's International Relations* (Routledge, 2012), 22–34.

In Saudi Arabia and Assadist Syria, where experts are less important and foreign policy-linked, knowledge-producing infrastructure is underdeveloped, media workers assume greater salience.[25] Entrusted with a propagandistic role aimed at explicating state foreign policy decisions to both domestic and foreign audiences, influential journalists and media commentators often function as conduits for reinforcing state narratives as well as signalling, and even testing, public receptivity to new foreign policy shifts and initiatives. In that sense, they act, much like their journalistic counterparts in the PRC, as the 'ears, eyes, throat and tongue of the Party' (*dǎng de ěr mù hóu shé*) – they speak within the parameters and interest-conceptions of the state.

By studying the narratives of the Chinese, Saudi, and Assadist Syrian foreign policy elites, we can obtain clues as to how their respective states locate and evaluate each other.[26] As we are specifically interested in those narratives generated from 2010 to 2023, a period coinciding, as already alluded to, with heightened perceptions of extensive change in the Middle East regional order, any investigation into these worldviews, as well as their synchroneities and disjunctions, could tell us much about where the region is potentially headed, and the PRC's evolving and anticipated role in this. That being said, we agree with Gary Sick's view:

> The future of the Persian Gulf and the wider Middle East is impossible to discern. But in any serious discussion of strategy, it is imperative to recognise that we are in uncharted waters, beset with Black Swans on all sides. Old formulas will not work and should be regarded with suspicion. The end of this process, to borrow a phrase from Shakespeare, will be unknown to the beginning.[27]

It is worth underscoring that this point is applicable not only to the distant and scholarly observers of the region but also to the elites in question, who have been blindsided by unexpected turns of events such as the overthrow of the Assadist regime by Hay'at Tahrīr al-Shām (HTS) in under two weeks. There are always omissions and missed variables in espoused worldviews,

---

[25] For a sense of the differences between Chinese and Arab knowledge-producing infrastructures, see Yanqiu Zheng, Guangshuo Yang, and Amira Elsherif, 'Asia-China Knowledge Networks: State of the Field', Social Science Research Council, 19 December 2022, 49–54, www.ssrc.org/publications/asia-china-knowledge-networks-state-of-the-field/.

[26] Jeffrey W. Legro, *Rethinking the World: Great Power Strategies and International Order* (Cornell University Press, 2007); Juliet Kaarbo, 'A Foreign Policy Analysis Perspective on the Domestic Politics Turn in IR Theory', *International Studies Review* 17, no. 2 (2015): 189–216.

[27] Gary Sick, 'A Plague of Black Swans in the Middle East', Lobelog, 24 February 2016, https://lobelog.com/a-plague-of-black-swans-in-the-middle-east/.

but regardless of the degree to which they miss or approximate grounded realities (with sometimes existentially costly results, as the Assadist regime learned), we can still get a sense of how the relevant actors understand their positionalities within the balance of power, what compels or constrains them, and their potential behaviour moving ahead. Put differently, narratives are like a cognitive map that can reveal to us the horizons of what is actionable (and likely) in minds of the elites – including whether the foreign policy elites of a Middle Eastern state (as an example) believe that an alliance with the PRC is desirable and within the realm of possibility, and whether their counterparts in Beijing, who are equally or more significant for such an outcome, would agree to such a proposal or not.

Our overall approach in this Element is inspired by Alexander Wendt's 'thin' constructivism, which recognises that 'brute material forces like biological needs, the physical environment, and technological artifacts do have intrinsic causal powers', whilst also acknowledging that it is only by considering the role of ideas, particularly those shared across purposive actors, that we can truly understand social life and the ways in which systems (or sub-systems) organise themselves.[28] For example, Chinese, Saudi, and Assadist Syrian elites all perceive the US as the most powerful actor in the Middle East due to its unbridled economic, technological, and military strength. Yet the specific role that is ascribed to Washington within the regional order, and thus how Beijing, Riyadh, and Damascus approach it (and in turn each other), varies depending on how these elites position themselves towards it, not only on geopolitical terms, but ideological ones as well.

Our attention to narratives deviates somewhat from the conventional approach that dominates the existing literature on Sino-Middle Eastern relations, and which mainly looks at the PRC's presence in the region through a realist (and often a reductionist and material-centric) lens ultimately concerned with US national interests (as broadly conceived) in the region. By centring the narratives of the relevant actors in our analysis, we provide new insights into how Chinese and local state actors conceive and debate their relationships on their own terms, free from the distortive prism of what Evan Feigenbaum has described as the 'strategic narcissism' of the great powers (in our case, the US).[29] A comparison of their worldviews can provide a more holistic view of where the divergences

---

[28] Alexander Wendt, *Social Theory of International Politics* (Cambridge University Press, 1999), 41.

[29] On the importance of this issue, see Tony Smith, 'New Bottles for New Wine: A Pericentric Framework for the Study of the Cold War', *Diplomatic History* 24, no. 4 (2000): 567–591;

and convergences lie between them, and what future for the Middle East has a greater likelihood of materialising as a result.³⁰ Put differently, what does the region actually look like from the vantage point of Beijing, and what does faraway China look like from regional capitals?

Our aim with this exercise is not to contest the findings of the existing scholarship per se but to complement and refine its interpretations of Sino-Middle East dynamics through an adjusted focus – that is, on the local, and within a comparative framework. This approach in and of itself is not novel and has been applied elsewhere with some success, whether in appraising PRC's entanglements in specific sectors in Africa and the Middle East, or in sketching (and anticipating) national trajectories, regional dynamics, and bilateral rivalries in other regions.³¹

We expect that a scrutinisation of these elites' narratives over the course of a decade will yield three possible scenarios on the nature and future of Sino-Middle Eastern relations.³² Under the first scenario, we would find that PRC, Saudi, and Assadist Syrian narratives, notwithstanding minor differences, share in a circumspect and reserved depiction of Chinese

---

Tim Sweijs and Michael J. Mazaar, 'Mind the Middle Powers', *War on the Rocks*, 4 April 2023, https://shorturl.at/Le257.

30 For an excellent piece of scholarship that examines how conflicting narratives have had a transformative impact on regional dynamics over the *longue durée*, see Michael N. Barnett, *Dialogues in Arab Politics: Negotiations in Regional Order* (Columbia University Press, Year, 1998); Evan Feigenbaum on X (formerly Twitter) 15 May 2024, https://x.com/EvanFeigenbaum/status/1790392876519629222.

31 Deborah Brautigam, *The Dragon's Gift: The Real Story of China in Africa* (Oxford University Press, 2009); Ching Kwan Lee, *The Specter of Global China: Politics, Labor, and Foreign Investments in Africa* (University of Chicago, 2017); Lina Benabdallah, *Shaping the Future of Power: Knowledge Production and Network-Building in China-Africa Relations* (University of Michigan Press, 2020); Amjed Rasheed, 'The Narrative of the Rise of China and Authoritarianism in the Global South: The Case of Egypt', *The International Spectator* 57, no. 2 (2022): 68–84; Benjamin Houghton, 'China's Balancing Strategy between Saudi Arabia and Iran: The View from Riyadh', *Asian Affairs* 53, no. 1: 124–144; Andrea Ghiselli and Mohammed Alsudairi, 'Exploiting China's Rise: Syria's Strategic Narrative and China's Participation in Middle Eastern Politics', *Global Policy* 14 (2023): 19–35; Daniel C. Lynch, *China's Futures: PRC Elites Debate Economics, Politics, and Foreign Policy* (Stanford University Press, 2015); the special issue introduced by Linus Hagstrom and Karl Gustafsson, 'Narrative Power: How Storytelling Shapes East Asian International Politics', *Cambridge Review of International Affairs* 32 (2019): 387–406; Banafsheh Keynoush and Edward Wastnidge, 'Narratives of Power Politics in the Iran–Saudi Relationship: The View from Tehran', in Edward Wastnidge and Simon Mabon (eds.), *Saudi Arabia and Iran: The Struggle to Shape the Middle East* (Manchester University Press, 2022), 33–54; Tobias Borck, *Seeking Stability Amidst Disorder: The Foreign Policies of Saudi Arabia, the UAE and Qatar, 2010–20* (Hurst, 2023).

32 Siegfried Schieder, 'New Institutionalism and Foreign Policy', in Klaus Brummer, Sebastian Harnisch, Kai Opperman, and Diana Panke (eds.), *Foreign Policy as Public Policy? Promises and Pitfalls* (Manchester University Press, 2019), 161–189.

involvement in regional governance and security. This would mean that the future of Sino-Middle Eastern ties is likely to be more of a stable continuation of what had existed since the late 1990s, with China being an important economic partner but little beyond that. The region might indeed be in the midst of a spasmic transition, and relations could very well continue to develop in strategic and sensitive sectors, but the PRC is neither expected by local state actors nor willing itself to assume a radically new role in that context.[33]

In the second scenario, Chinese, Saudi, and Assadist Syrian narratives have co-evolved towards a new consensus wherein they all anticipate greater and unprecedented PRC engagement in regional governance and security issues. Such a discursive shift and alignment would therefore confirm that the 2010s does indeed mark the beginnings of unprecedented Chinese 'embedding' in the Middle East. The PRC's actions, encompassing the establishment of a support base (bǎozhàng jīdì) in Djibouti in 2017, the launching of the Middle East Security Forum (2019–), and its mediational brokerage of the Saudi–Iranian détente in 2023, could therefore be re-interpreted as concrete expressions of a new era of Chinese hegemony that will only become more apparent as the years progress.

The third and final scenario would feature narratives out of synch with one another, with discordant perceptions of the regional order and China's place within it. While the old patterns of behaviour are no longer sustainable or desirable, new ones have yet to emerge, meaning that a high degree of uncertainty and fluidity continues to hover over Sino-Middle Eastern relations. In such a scenario, and depending on the narrational compositions of the different foreign policy elites, the PRC might be attempting to carve a 'sphere of influence' in a resistant and unwilling region, or regional actors are engaged in playing the 'China card' against one another or in order to gain leverage vis-à-vis other external great powers, laying diplomatic traps in turn for a reluctant Beijing. In the words of neo-institutionalist scholars, the 2010s would be the beginning of a long and ongoing temporal separation between two different eras – an interregnum with no end in sight, and where the terrain of possibility is constantly shifting.[34]

---

[33] Colley, 'A Post-American Middle East?'
[34] Giovanni Capoccia and R. Daniel Kelemen, 'The Study of Critical Junctures: Theory, Narrative, and Counterfactuals in Historical Institutionalism', *World Politics* 59, no. 3 (April 2007): 341–369; Paul Pierson, *Politics in Time: History, Institutions, and Social Analysis* (Princeton University Press, 2004).

On the Case Studies

What underpins our case selections? While the raison d'être for examining PRC narratives is obvious, focusing on those of Saudi Arabia and Assadist Syria out of many other important players in the Middle East, such as Algeria, Egypt, Türkiye, Iran, and Israel, is less clear. It would have certainly been ideal to incorporate more case studies, but an Element of this length has forced us to be more discerning. We took two variables into account when selecting for the case studies: the inherent tangible and intangible capabilities of a state on the one hand; and the relations it maintains with the current regional hegemon – the US – on the other. The logic for this is quite straightforward: the sum of the economic, diplomatic, and military capacities of a given state informs the options of a foreign policy elite vis-à-vis the regional order and the extent to which it can engage and play the external powers against one another. Close alignment with (or distance from) the US structures the positionalities of nearly all states in the Middle East and has multi-scalar implications for their domestic and foreign policies. The confluence of these two variables functions as a material force that moulds the narratives justifying and guiding foreign policy elite perspectives on the regional order and the PRC's potential place within it, now and into the future.

In terms of capabilities, Saudi Arabia can be described as a historical middle power in the Middle East, a status accrued from its custodial control (and thus religious soft power) of the sacred sites of Islam (Makkah and Madinah) and its possession of the region's largest economy (at USD $1.07 trillion as of 2023).[35] Much of this has been due to the Kingdom being one of the world's largest hydrocarbon producers, providing it with immense wealth and leverage. Under Crown Prince Mohammed bin Salman (2017–), the nature of Saudi power has changed in the 2010s. Considerable resources have been channelled to support wide-ranging economic and social reforms under the National Transformation Plan and the forging of a new Saudi nationalism – all geared towards changing the rentierist political economy of the country.[36] Concurrently, Saudi elites have embraced an activist foreign policy that has oscillated between aggressive (and unprecedented) military intervention to the

---

[35] 'Saudi Arabia', World Bank Group, undated, https://data.worldbank.org/country/saudi-arabia?view=chart.

[36] For analysis on recent developments in Saudi Arabia, see Madawi Al-Rasheed (ed.), *Salman's Legacy: The Dilemmas of a New Era in Saudi Arabia* (Oxford University Press, 2018); David Ottaway, *Mohammed Bin Salman: The Icarus of Saudi Arabia?* (Lynne Rienner, 2021).

more recent pursuit of détentes with erstwhile rivals. The departure from a longstanding conservative modality of governance and diplomacy, and the perceived increase in the country's influence, has led some regional observers to proclaim that the Saudi leadership is inaugurating the 'fourth Saudi state' (*al-dawla al-suʻudiyya al-rābiʻa*) and spearheading, to quote the Emirati scholar Abdullah Abdulkhaleq, the 'Gulf's (ascendant) moment in Arab history'.[37] Accordingly, and with an eye towards the decade-long span we are interested in, the Kingdom emerges as an ambitious actor with significant political and financial resources to affect not only regional events but also the contours of its relationship with the PRC.

Assadist Syria's situation was, up to its demise, the complete opposite in every sense possible. During its heyday under Hafiz al-Assad (1971–2000), the country was akin to an aspirational middle power in Middle East that relied on shrewd pragmatic diplomacy to balance against different actors and to even exercise some degree of hegemony over neighbouring Lebanon.[38] Since 2011, it experienced a loss of popular support, territorial fragmentation, intervention by foreign actors and proxies, and near-catastrophic economic and demographic collapse under an all-out civil war and predatory economic behaviour by its ruling elites – effectively rendering Syria a failed state.[39] Though the regime appeared to have weathered the harrowing challenge of the past decade, and was until recently undergoing a slow process of regional rehabilitation – with re-admission into the Arab League and the re-opening of the Saudi embassy in Damascus – Syria entered the 2020s as

---

[37] The fourth Saudi state was a term first popularised by the Lebanon-based Saudi commentator Ahmad 'Adnan to describe a blueprint for reforming the Kingdom, but which was later widely invoked by other Saudi scholars and observers since 2015 with the ascension of King Salman to the throne; see Ahmad 'Adnan, *al-Suʻudiyya al-badila: malamih al-dawla al-rabiʻa* ('The alternative Saudi: signs of the fourth state') (Beirut: al-Tanwir, 2012); Rotana Khalijiyya, 'Al-doktor Ahmad al-Tuweijri: al-malik Salman bin Abdulaziz huwa muasis al-dawla al-suʻudiyya al-rabiʻa' ('Dr Ahmed al-Tuweijri: King Salman is the founder of the fourth Saudi state') (YouTube), 13 February 2015, www.youtube.com/watch?v=FTp0tikY5zI; Abdulkhaleq Abdullah, *Lahdhat al-khalij fi al-tarikh al-ʻarabi al-muʻasir* ('The Gulf moment in contemporary Arab history') (Dar al-Farabi, 2018).

[38] Hinnebusch Raymond, 'Pax-Syriana? The Origins, Causes and Consequences of Syria's Role in Lebanon', *Mediterranean Politics* 3, no. 1 (1998): 137–160.

[39] For data on the developmental regression in Syria, see 'The World Bank in Syria – Overview', World Bank Group, undated, www.worldbank.org/en/country/syria/overview; for a sense of the moral tragedy that has befallen Syria for the last decade, see the interview with the Syrian political dissident Yassin al-Haj Saleh: Nisrin al-Zahr and Catherine Kukiyu, 'Al-ʻalam min mandhur Suri' ('The world from a Syrian viewpoint'), *al-Jumhuriyya*, 5 April 2022, https://shorturl.at/8oeRm.

a fractured, sanctioned, devastated, and impoverished polity.[40] According to the United Nations High Commissioner for Refugees (UNHCR), as of 2022, nearly a quarter of Syria's population (5.2 million) continued to seek asylum in neighbouring countries, and a somewhat larger figure (6.8 million) is estimated to have been internally displaced.[41] Its economy was a shambles, with World Bank estimates indicating that it had contracted since 2010 by 84 per cent, standing in 2022 at around USD $23 billion, barely half that of neighbouring Jordan.[42] Capabilities-wise, Assadist Syria was a shell with barely any resources to spare: it could not affect regional events in a proactive sense and was reduced primarily to an arena for different contending actors to pursue their strategic interests.

Turning to the second variable, that of relations with the US,[43] Saudi Arabia and Assadist Syria have historically positioned themselves, in both the Cold War and post-Cold War eras, within diametrically opposed camps concerning the regional order.[44] The Kingdom has long presented itself as

---

[40] 'Saudi Foreign Minister: Syria Could Return to Arab League, but Not Yet', *Reuters*, 8 March 2023, www.reuters.com/world/middle-east/saudi-foreign-minister-syria-could-return-arab-league-not-yet-2023-03-07/; Laila Bassam and Aziz El Yaakoubi, 'After Iran, Saudi Arabia to Re-establish Ties with Syria, Sources Say', *Reuters*, 23 March 2023, https://shorturl.at/Q6e7q.

[41] 'Syria Emergency', UNHCR, www.unhcr.org/emergencies/syria-emergency.

[42] 'Syrian Arab Republic', World Bank Group, undated, https://data.worldbank.org/country/syrian-arab-republic; 'Jordan', World Bank Group, undated, https://data.worldbank.org/country/jordan.

[43] As with the US, both states have had divergent histories of bilateral relations with the PRC that continue to inform, albeit faintly, the framing of their present-day discourses about China. Syria was one of the first Arab states to extend diplomatic recognition to the PRC in August 1956, and notwithstanding periods of bilateral acrimony and tension that were aggravated by later Ba'athist alignment with the Soviet Union, maintained relatively friendly ties with the PRC. Saudi Arabia, by contrast, was closely aligned with anti-communist states in East Asia, most prominently the Republic of China (Taiwan), for much of the Cold War. Though Sino-Saudi relations started to thaw in the 1980s, it was only in July 1990 that relations were officially inaugurated, effectively making Saudi Arabia the last Arab state to recognise the PRC. In the post-Cold War decades that followed, this dichotomy has only deepened, though in an inverse direction: as Saudi Arabia transformed into one of the PRC's most significant comprehensive strategic partners in the Middle East, and is actively courted and visited by the highest echelons of the Chinese leadership, Syria has become something of an afterthought, only gaining a strategic appellation for the bilateral relationship – per the lexicon of the PRC Ministry of Foreign Affairs (MFA) – in 2023. See Mohammed Turki Alsudairi, 'Forging an Anti-Bandung: Saudi Arabia and East Asia's Cold War', *Comparative Studies of South Asia, Africa, and the Middle East* 43, no. 3 (2023): 412–426; The Ministry of Foreign Affairs of the People's Republic of China, 'Zhongguo tong shate de guanxi', April 2024, https://short-link.me/14jw9; The Ministry of Foreign Affairs of the People's Republic of China, 'Zhongguo tong shuliya de guanxi', April 2024, https://shorturl.at/BqOYK.

[44] This is an over-simplification as both countries developed a relatively high degree of cooperation between them that transcended, for a time, these campist alignments;

being part of a US-leaning, status quo-supporting 'axis of moderation' (*mihwar al-iʿtidāl*) in the (Arab) Middle East comprised of the Arab monarchies and Egypt, and which together stand against a succession of de-stabilising actors ranging from Islamist Iran to the short-lived Dāʿishī Caliphate (also known as the Islamic State of Iraq and the Levant; ISIL).[45] Assadist Syria, by contrast, identified itself with an altogether different and opposing camp, the 'axis of resistance' (*mihwar al-muqāwamah*), an amalgam of excluded regimes (Iran and the Houthī in Yemen) and sub-state actors or proxies (including Hizbollah in Lebanon and an assortment of political parties and militias in Iraq) that have actively contested US and Israeli hegemony, and which also view themselves in confrontation with the axis of moderation.[46] On a different and higher scale, but one still relevant to these positionalities, the regime has closely aligned itself with, and has drawn patronage and support from, Russia (in both its Soviet and post-Soviet iterations), placing it for all intents and purposes within an anti-American sphere of influence. The half-century-old Russian military naval base in Tartus, established in 1971, is the most concrete expression of this alignment.[47]

Considering these variables, Saudi Arabia and Assadist Syria clearly stand at opposite ends of the two spectrums. With a Wendtian perspective in mind, they have the potential to provide insights into the full range of narratives circulating in the Middle East about the future of the regional order and the PRC's place within it. We do not claim they exhaust all possibilities, stances, and attitudes, but they do supply, as opposite poles, most of the narrational strands found elsewhere in the region. Virtually all countries in the region, we would argue, fall somewhere between their two extremes. The usefulness of the Saudi–Syria juxtaposition has been

---

see Francesco Belcastro, 'An Odd "Foreign Policy Couple"? Syria and Saudi Arabia 1970–1989', *Journal of Balkan and Near Eastern Studies* 22, no. 1 (2020): 29–46.

[45] The term was widely used throughout the Saudi press in the mid 2010s. For some examples, see Muhammad Jazairi, '"Mihwar al-itidal 2" fi muqabil muhwar "al-muqawamah al-taifi"' ('"Axis of Moderation 2" versus the "Sectarian Axis of Resistance"'), *Eleqtisadiyya*, 16 March 2014, www.aleqt.com/2014/03/16/article_833631.html; Raed Omari, 'The "Arab Axis of Moderation" Needs Help', Alarabiya, 27 September 2013, https://short-link.me/10d28.

[46] Syria has long been in the practice of embracing region-wide rejectionist roles. Following Anwar al-Sadat's visit to Jerusalem in November 1977, it formed, along with several other states and organisations, a short-lived 'steadfastness and confrontation front' (*jabhat al-ṣumūd wal tahadī*); see Patrick Seale, *Asad: The Struggle for the Middle East* (University of California Press, 1989), 311.

[47] Edward Delman, 'The Link between Putin's Military Campaigns in Syria and Ukraine', *The Atlantic*, 2 October 2015, www.theatlantic.com/international/archive/2015/10/navy-base-syria-crimea-putin/408694/.

used in other works that have sought to explore issues such as threat perception and alliance-making in the region.[48] And, indeed, this partially explains why we continue to look at Assadist Syria, despite its 'extinction', when thinking about Sino-Middle Eastern futures: its views about the regional order and the PRC overlap with those of other state and sub-state actors in the region that share in its variable positionalities (for instance, Houthī-ruled Yemen), though perhaps not with those of its successors(s), such as the HTS.[49] Hence, as we indicate in the conclusion, we believe it is possible to extrapolate from the Saudi and Assadist Syrian cases to make informed speculations about Sino-Middle Eastern relations.

On the Sources

We used a diverse set of authoritative sources in examining the narratives of foreign policy elites. For political and bureaucratic elites in all three selected cases, we analysed Chinese- and Arabic-language material gathered from official portals, such as the Xinhua News Agency (XNA), the Saudi Press Agency (SPA), and the Syrian Arab News Agency (SANA). We paid special attention to the statements made by political leaders, foreign ministers, and diplomats about the regional order and the PRC for 2010–2023. This is particularly true for Assadist Syria, where the leadership had been active in commenting about its relationship with the PRC (Figure 1). We supplemented these with material gathered from the websites of the three countries' ministries of foreign affairs, as well as with interviews given by these elites to the media (local or international). Though there are problems with taking statements from official sources at face value, we firmly believe that they are important in discerning state-level signalling and interpretations of events – in sum, their worldviews.

Regarding communication elites who 'mirror' foreign policy thinking, we tried to be sensitive to the differences and source availability across the Chinese, Saudi, and Assadist Syrian discursive environments. For the PRC, we examined the works of scholars who were involved in the production of knowledge about the Middle East, with an eye towards supporting or fine-tuning the state's foreign policy there.[50] We specifically looked at publications

---

[48] May Darwich, *Threats and Alliances in the Middle East: Saudi and Syrian Policies in a Turbulent Region* (Cambridge University Press, 2019).

[49] Up to the moment of writing, the HTS-led transitional authorities appear committed to a total recalibration of Syria's foreign policy, rejecting traditional alignment with Iran and its allies, and courting support from Türkiye, the GCC, and the West.

[50] Anyone familiar with Chinese scholarship cannot but notice that most academic articles published in the PRC are akin to policy briefs, with many including specific policy

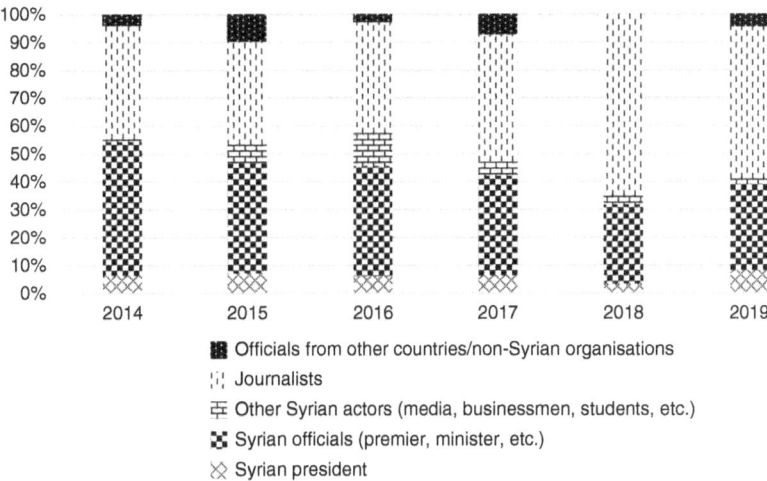

Figure 1 Who talks about China?
Note: The figure reflects a calculation of 583 English-language SANA articles produced between 2014 and 2019. The number of articles attributed to 'journalists' refer to those in which no specific Syrian person was quoted commenting on the PRC.
Source: Authors.

that appeared in journals managed by major state-affiliated think tanks and research centres concerned with the Middle East, most notably *Arab World Studies* (*ālābó shìjiè yánjiū*) and *West Asia and Africa* (*xīyǎ fēizhōu*).[51] To ensure that we captured a representative slice of the debate, we included articles on the Middle East found in five top Chinese-language international relations journals: *World Economics and Politics* (*shìjiè jīngjì yǔ zhèngzhì*), *Foreign Affairs Review* (*wàijiāo pínglùn*), *Contemporary International Relations* (*xiàndài guójì guānxì*), *Global Review* (*guójì zhǎnwàng*), and *International Studies* (*guójì wèntí yánjiū*).[52] In addition to these academic

---

recommendations. For a discussion on how Middle East studies in the PRC is tied to policymaking, see Ghiselli, *Protecting China's Interests Overseas*, 114–143. Of course, the linkage between academia and policymaking, and the former's capacity to reshape the latter, is by no means a Chinese phenomenon. For examples, see Robert Vitalis, *White World Order, Black Power Politics: The Birth of American International Relations* (Cornell University Press, 2018); David Brenner and Enze Han, 'Forgotten Conflicts: Producing Knowledge and Ignorance in Security Studies', *Journal of Global Security Studies* 7, no. 1, 2022.

[51] These journals are, respectively, affiliated with the Middle East Studies Institute of Shanghai International Studies University and the Institute of West Asian and African Studies at the Chinese Academy of Social Sciences (CASS) in Beijing. CASS is overseen by the PRC State Council, the highest administrative body in the country.

[52] These journals are published, respectively, by the CASS Institute of World Economics and Politics, the MFA-affiliated Foreign Affairs University, the Ministry of State Security-affiliated China Institute of Contemporary International Relations (CICIR), the Shanghai Institute for

journals, we also examined articles and interviews by Chinese experts from PRC media outlets such as the *People's Daily* (*rénmín rìbào*), the *Global Times* (*huánqiú shíbào*), *The Paper* (*péngpài xīnwén*), and XNA's *Globe* (*huánqiú*).

As for Saudi Arabia and Assadist Syria, we looked at a different set of sources to reconstruct the thinking among foreign policy elites.[53] This is because a sizable area studies knowledge-producing infrastructure tied to policymaking circles is absent or still in the process of being built, a phenomenon that holds true for much of the Arab world.[54] What these two cases do have are state-directed/controlled media ecosystems which, much like those of the PRC, not only disseminate official thinking on foreign policy but also serve to 'test the waters' on new policies and re-shape public opinion on key issues.[55] However, there are nuanced variations and challenges, rooted in political and economic differences, between the two cases that must be taken into account. Nearly all major print and digital media in Syria, such as *al-Baʿath* (the ruling party's mouthpiece), *Athawra*, and *Tishrīn*, were under the direct purview of the Ministry of Information, ensuring active censorship and monitoring of content in ways dovetailing with state interests.[56] This control was buttressed further by tight legislation, as well as by the strict socialisation of media workers into operating within the red lines of the regime.[57] The media in Syria for

---

International Studies (SIIS), and the MFA-affiliated China Institute of International Studies. SIIS has formal channels for the transmission of internal reports to the Chinese central government and is close to both the MFA and the Shanghai municipal government.

[53] For Saudi Arabia, we could have opted to look at articles published by *The Diplomat* (*al-Diblumāsī*) and *The Journal of International Studies* (*Majalat al-dirāsāt al-duwaliyya*), both of which are affiliated with the MFA-attached Prince Saud Al-Faisal Institute for Diplomatic Studies. However, electronically available issues were sporadic and did not cover the period 2010–2023 in any consistent manner.

[54] This situation has been changing in Saudi Arabia over the course of the past decade. State demand for locally produced research, as well as increased (government) funding sources, has fuelled the proliferation of new think tanks and research centres (including some with no public profile). This development remains nascent, however. For one view, see Mona Ali, 'Gulf Think Tanks and Regional Security Policy after 2011' in Md. Muddassir Quamar (ed), *Politics of Change in Middle East and North Africa since Arab Spring* (Routledge, 2022), 70–90.

[55] For instances of this, see Lisa Blaydes, 'Authoritarian Media and Diversionary Threats: Lessons from 30 Years of Syrian State Discourse', *Political Science Research and Methods* 9, no. 4 (2021): 693–708; Frances Yaping Wang, 'Barking without Biting: Understanding Chinese Media Campaigns during Foreign Policy Disputes', *Security Studies* 30, no. 4 (2021): 517–549.

[56] The exception perhaps is Al-Mayadeen, a privately owned TV network based in Lebanon but which, for whatever monetary or ideological reasons, takes a pro-regime stance in its coverage.

[57] 'Syria', Media Landscapes, https://medialandscapes.org/country/syria/policies/media-legislation.

all intents and purposes followed the classic mode of being a party-state echo chamber. This creates a strong temptation to throw an undifferentiating net in approaching these sources, and as a result we decided to give more weight to the interviews and speeches of Syrian leaders themselves. This was guided by the fact that they were simply more numerous and accessible than their PRC or Saudi equivalents: the Syrian Presidency YouTube channel, for example, uploaded well over twenty interviews (each exceeding twenty minutes in length) of Bashar al-Assad with the foreign media in the 2010s. This accomplishes our objective in outlining the worldview of the foreign policy elites, at the apex of which sits leaders like al-Assad whom the media ecosystem serves.

Saudi Arabia, by comparison, has leveraged its vast resources since the 1970s to establish a pan-Arab media empire that has succeeded in heavily influencing (albeit not fully dominating) Arabosphere cultural and ideological spaces.[58] The Saudi Research and Media Group and Middle East Broadcasting – both linked to regime-aligned networks – have played a critical role in this regard, founding several well-known outlets, such as *Asharq al-Awsat* and *Alarabiyya*. Under Crown Prince Mohammed bin Salman, the media's significance has only deepened. Some of the (former) editors of these outlets have recently assumed important state positions, including ambassadorial and ministerial postings. Because of the various linkages tying these outlets to the Saudi state, many of the journalists and commentators and especially those in editorial capacities with longstanding experiences in the field – act as explainers and advocates for national policies. In some cases, as exemplified by Abdulrahman al-Rashid and his weekly column in *Asharq al-Awsat*, they can provide insights into the thinking of the regime. Accordingly, we were more selective with the sources we examined for the Saudi communication elites, emphasising columns and pieces written by current and former editors at the two Saudi newspapers listed. We also draw on the works of a small grouping of scholars embedded within various Saudi think tanks and institutes which have gained newfound patronage from the state.

It is important to emphasise that we primarily focus on Chinese and Arabic language sources. This is because it is frequently the case that the content of the articles published in English by Chinese and Arab media and

---

[58] On Saudi domination of classical media spheres, see Andrew Hammond, 'Saudi Arabia's Media Empire: Keeping the Masses at Home', Arab Media & Society, 1 October 2007, https://short-link.me/10d2y; on its more recent forays into social media networks, see Marc Owen Jones, *Digital Authoritarianism in the Middle East: Deception, Disinformation and Social Media* (Hurst Publishers, 2022).

elites is strategically produced to be appealing to a Western readership. Key ideas and concepts that compose the worldviews of Chinese and Arab elites might be omitted because they are difficult to translate into English or because they are politically unpalatable to Western readers.

On the Breakdown of the Sections

The Element is comprised of four sections. The first three are dedicated, respectively, to examining the evolving narratives surrounding the Middle East's regional order and China's place within it in the PRC, Saudi Arabia, and Assadist Syria. Each section analyses the discourse generated by the foreign policy elites of these three states, highlighting recurrent themes and ideas, over the period 2010 to 2023. At times, the discussion might reference key events or developments to clarify whether changes happened only at the rhetorical level or were matched by policy actions. The final fourth section presents and generalises our findings to produce broader insights into Sino-Middle Eastern relations. It dwells upon the core question of whether the 2010s can be considered a transformative juncture in Sino-Middle Eastern relations and considers some of the variables that might impact the trajectory of these relations in the coming decades.

China: Adjusting to a Changing Regional Order

This section examines how the changes in the Middle East regional order, and the PRC's place within it as an extra-regional great power, have been perceived by Chinese foreign policy elites. For much of the 2010s, many of them assessed the region to be one plagued by extreme volatility, a situation they attributed to bad governance and economic mismanagement among local state actors, irrational rivalries between them, and recurrent Western (American) intervention. A cautious optimism started to appear among these elites between the end of that decade and the early 2020s as they increasingly took note of how leading actors, especially GCC member-states such as Saudi Arabia and the United Arab Emirates, began to adjust their domestic and foreign policy priorities towards intra-regional cooperation and economic development, and, as a consequence of that, have become somewhat less dependent on the US. However, the elites anticipate that the path to genuine multilateralism and greater regional integration will be a difficult and arduous one, and older and more destructive patterns of region-wide politics will endure for some time to come – a more promising Middle Eastern future is, in their eyes, still elusive and 'under construction'.

With the region amidst what they interpret to be a drawn-out interregnum, Chinese foreign policy elites are cautious about how the PRC should position itself. The vast majority show little appetite for radical adjustments or wholesale involvement there, at least in the political and military sense. This conservatism, which has long characterised the PRC's approach to the Middle East, suggests that there are yet to be any compelling reasons to re-shape Chinese foreign policy, especially if their national interests, however understood, continue to be safeguarded. While the PRC might try to experiment with new ways to refine its engagement with the region, seizing opportunities whenever they might arise, the internal discussions within the PRC hint at a continuation of what had prevailed in the past: the PRC will remain a transactional extra-regional power that stands, for the most part, aloof from (and guarded about) substantively enmeshing itself in the regional order and its security architecture. When considering these debates, it is clear that emulating the hegemonic role of the US in the Middle East is not even an afterthought, let alone an idealised endpoint.

Looking at a Turbulent Region

Since the eruption of the Arab Spring, Chinese foreign policy elites have attributed the central causes of regional turmoil to bad governance, coupled with a neglect of economic development. According to Niu Xinchun, the former director of the China Institutes of Contemporary International Relations (CICIR), who is now based at Ningxia University, many countries in the region failed to find, and embrace, a sustainable political-economic model, leading in turn to the uprisings of 2010–2011.[59] In the words of Gong Xiaosheng, China's Special Envoy to the Middle East (2014–2019): 'unbalanced development has caused social turmoil or even civil strife, and civil strife and social turmoil have made development more difficult, and the exploration of new paths more challenging'.[60] At a deeper level, these failures stem from the fractured nature of many regional governments, dominated as they are by interest groups that form a deep state preventing the normal evolution of state and societal institutions.[61] This overall

---

[59] Xinchun Niu, 'Jiětǐ de zhōngdōng chóng huí "ruò zhǔquán shídài"' ('A collapsing Middle East: the return to an "era of weak sovereignty"'), *Contemporary International Relations* 7 (2017): 1–4.
[60] Xiaosheng Gong, 'Zhōngdōng de rèdiǎn wèntí yǔ zhōngguó de zhōngdōng wàijiāo' ('The hot spots of the Middle East and China's Middle East diplomacy'), *Foreign Affairs* 126 (2017), www.cpifa.org/cms/book/113.
[61] A similar argument can also be found in Jian Wang, 'Cóng bā yǐ chōngtú tòuxī zhōngdōng zhèngzhì dòngdàng de gēnyuán' ('Insights into the origins of turmoil in the Middle East from the analysis of the Israeli–Palestinian issue'), *West Asia and Africa* 2 (2015): 35–57.

situation, this line of thought goes, has severely undermined the capacity of these states to resolve popular unrest (as shown by the long-shadow of the Arab Spring) and counteract internal and external subversive influences, leading many Chinese foreign policy elites to deem the Middle East as having entered an 'era of weak sovereignty' (*ruò zhǔquán shídài*). Yang Fuchang, an expert at the China Foundation for International Studies who served as ambassador in many Middle Eastern countries and vice minister of foreign affairs in charge of that region during the early 1990s, asserts as much in his analysis.[62]

These problems are compounded by the imbalances of power that exist between the different states, leading to an unstable regional order.[63] Among the Arab countries, the GCC member-states have significantly expanded their influence, while traditional powers such as Egypt and Iraq have declined. The relations between Arab and non-Arab countries, too, are unbalanced, with Israel, Türkiye, and Iran becoming more assertive following the US pivot away from the Middle East under the Obama administration – a phenomenon that has been dubbed American 'strategic contraction' (*zhànlüè shōusuō*) by Chinese scholars.[64] With the conclusion of the Joint Comprehensive Plan of Action (JCPOA) in July 2015, there was a very strong expectation in the PRC that Iran would emerge as the most prominent regional power: Hua Liming, a retired senior Chinese diplomat, made this argument, for example, in an article published in *Foreign Affairs*, a journal overseen by the Chinese People's Institute of Foreign Affairs.[65] The decreasing interest, and willingness, of the US to sustain the existing regional order has likewise created an opening for extra-regional actors such as Russia to intervene, thereby drawing the Middle East into the broader global struggle between the great powers.[66]

---

[62] Fuchang Yang, 'Zhōngdōng dà guīmó dòngdàng yǔ wǒguó de wàijiāo yìngduì' ('Large-scale instability in the Middle East and China's diplomatic reaction'), *Arab World Studies* 3 (2012): 3–11.

[63] Bingbing Wu, 'Zhōngdōng zhànlüè géjú shīhéng yǔ zhōngguó de zhōngdōng zhànlüè' ('The Middle East's unbalanced structure and China's Middle East strategy'), *Foreign Affairs Review* 30, no. 6 (2013): 35–48; Bingbing Wu, 'Zhōngdōng zhànlüè géjú yǔ biànhuà shìjiè zhōng de zhōngdōng' ('The strategic structure and the Middle East in a changing world'), *World Knowledge* 3 (2021): 14–17.

[64] For example: Weijian Li, 'Dāngqián zhōngdōng ānquán júshì jí duì zhōngguó zhōngdōng wàijiāo de yǐngxiǎng' ('The current Middle Eastern security situation and implications for China's Middle East diplomacy'), *Global Review* 3 (2014): 22–34, 154–155.

[65] Liming Hua, 'Duì dāngqián zhōngdōng júshì de jǐ diǎn kànfǎ' ('Some thoughts about the current situation in the Middle East'), *Foreign Affairs* 118 (2015), www.cpifa.org/cms/book/8.

[66] Andrea Ghiselli, 'An Opportunistic Russia in the Middle East, a View from China', *Cambridge Review of International Affairs* 37, no. 2 (2023): 163–181.

Notwithstanding these negative assessments, Chinese foreign policy elites have expressed optimistic views of the region and its future, especially from the mid 2010s. The *Arab Policy Paper* published by the PRC government in 2016 emphasised that 'currently, Arab states are independently exploring the development paths suited to their own national realities. They are committed to pursuing industrialisation, enhancing employment and improving people's livelihood. They are active in promoting peace and stability in the region and are playing important roles in regional and international affairs.'[67] Chinese experts have echoed similar perspectives. Feng Lulu, the vice dean of the China Institute of Arab States Studies at Ningxia University, argued in 2020 that the Middle East was now on its way to adopting the hallmarks of modernity – industrialisation, nationalism, and secularism – after decades of being an 'anti-modernisation' (*fǎn xiàndàihuà*) outlier due to Western colonialism and interventionism.[68] Such shifts, he claims, were enabled by the decreasing price of oil, the waning influence of religion, growing Arab acceptance of Israel, and the gradual withdrawal of the US. Concerning the last point, many Chinese experts perceive, and welcome, a trend among local state actors for 'diplomatic diversification' (*wàijiāo duōyuán huà*) away from the US.[69] The latter trend has been mostly associated with the GCC member-states.[70]

There is an awareness that these developments will take time to mature, and the process will by no means be smooth or straightforward as many local state actors have to contend with many of the structural problems and region-wide imbalances mentioned earlier. There are always crises that risk flaring up at any given moment, reversing the progress made. The Palestinian–Israeli conflict, despite its marginalisation in regional politics (and signs of mounting normalisation) up until Hamas' attack on Israel in October 2023, is one demonstrative example: An Huihou, a former ambassador serving as director of the Strategic Studies Centre of

---

[67] The State Council of the People's Republic of China, 'Zhongguo dui alabo guojia zhengce wenjian (quanwen)'.

[68] Lulu Feng, 'Zhōngdōng shèhuì fāzhǎn wèntí jí qí zhìlǐ fāng'àn zōng lùn' ('A discussion of the development problems of the Middle East and their solutions'), *Arab World Studies* 5 (2020): 126–142, 160.

[69] Fan Zhang, 'Hǎiwān jūnzhǔguó duì zhōngdōng guójiā duìwài yuánzhù dòngyīn de fā zhǎn biànhuà' ('The evolution of the drivers behind the Gulf monarchies' foreign aid to Middle East countries'), *West Asia and Africa* 1 (2016): 145–160; Jian Wang, 'Zhōngdōng dìyuán zhèngzhì géjú biànhuà yǔ zhōng ā jīngmào fāzhǎn chángyuǎn zhànlüè' ('The changes in the geopolitical situation in the Middle East and the long-term strategy for the development of Sino-Arab trade'), *West Asia and Africa* 3 (2014): 48–64.

[70] Enrico Fardella and Andrea Ghiselli, *Power Shifts? China's Growing Influence in the Gulf: Key Trends and Regional Debates in 2023* (T.wai, 2024), 10–11.

the China Institute of International Studies' Foundation for International Studies, voiced this perspective in his analysis from 2017.[71] This reading could be discerned also from the response of Foreign Minister Wang Yi to a journalist from *al-Jazeera* during the press conference for the fifth session of the Twelfth National People's Congress in early March that same year: he asserted that the region was 'at a critical crossroads, where there is both the risk of increased unrest and the hope of ushering in peace'.[72]

From these snippets, it is clear that Chinese foreign policy elites are united in their vision of the Middle East in the 2010s as an extremely turbulent region that is still in the midst of re-ordering itself, though the endpoint of this process remains unclear. While PRC media usually attributes this regional turbulence to the negative role of foreign powers such as the US, it is evident that these elites hold a more nuanced view: instability is understood to be rooted in local failures at governance, on the one hand, and the absence of a stable balance of power at the regional level, on the other.[73] The most likely explanation for this discrepancy is that the media in the PRC are not really meant to host a discussion or debate on such issues but to communicate specific political interpretations of the events to the general public. At the same time, Chinese foreign policy elites are reservedly optimistic in so far as they see a silver lining to the situation, identifying positive trends that might contribute to the emergence of a more stable regional order at some point in the future.

Core or 'Normal' Interests?

Chinese foreign policy elites have long debated the nature and strategic relevance of the PRC's interests in the Middle East.[74] Although there is little doubt that the country has proliferating interests in the region, their relative weight in comparison with those in other parts of the world has been subject to some contestation within the PRC. Niu Xinchun, who has written prolifically on this topic throughout the 2010s, concluded that the country's overall interests in the Middle East are best

---

[71] Huihou An, 'Zhōngdōng géjú biànhuà jiākuài' ('The change of the situation in the Middle East is speeding up)', *Foreign Affairs* 123 (2017), www.cpifa.org/cms/book/95.

[72] 'Middle East Situation at Crucial Crossroads: Chinese FM', Xinhua, 8 March 2017, www.xinhuanet.com//english/2017-03/08/c_136112526.htm.

[73] This divergence can be noted in the monthly reviews of the Chinese media discourse on the Middle East and North Africa published by the ChinaMed Project; see www.chinamed.it/chinamed-observer.

[74] For an overview of the debate, see Ghiselli, *Protecting China's Interests Overseas*, 114–143.

conceived as 'normal' (*yībān*) when compared to elsewhere.[75] Any threats to them – arising from regional turmoil, for example – could be potentially costly in economic and political terms, but they would be unable to fundamentally undermine the national and regime security of the PRC. This interpretation is confirmed by recent analysis of the PRC's Middle East policy and discourse carried out by Zhang Chuchu, a rising expert at Fudan University in Shanghai, who concluded that the region has long been 'a second or third-order concern for Chinese policymakers'.[76]

Although this may come off as surprising, the Middle East – per Niu – is a somewhat marginal region in terms of the PRC's global economic interests. Though the region was in the 1980s a crucial market for Chinese construction companies, and thus an important source of much needed hard currency for the PRC,[77] that is no longer the case (Figure 2). Additionally, while Chinese products are increasingly popular, the Middle East is not a major destination for Chinese exports either (Figure 3). The region has been a major source of energy for the PRC since the 1990s (Figure 4), but those imports are not under threat.[78] Other scholars have written that Chinese investment in the region could be at risk because of possible terrorist attacks or American interference.[79] Yet the data supports Niu's basic contention: although Chinese investments in the region have increased in absolute value (Figure 5), they have decreased in relation to the PRC's global capital footprint (Figure 6). Moreover, such investments are mostly concentrated in stable countries such as those of the GCC member-states (Figure 7). The risk of militant spillovers affecting China's Xinjiang Uygur

---

[75] Xinchun Niu, 'Zhōngguó zài zhōngdōng de lìyì yǔ yǐngxiǎng lì fēnxī' ('An analysis of Chinese interests and influence in the Middle East'), *Contemporary International Relations* 10 (2013): 44–52, 68; Xinchun Niu, 'Zhōngguó yǔ zhōngdōng: Xīn wèntí, xīn shìjiǎo, xīn fāngfǎ' ('China and the Middle East: new problems, new perspectives, new methods'), *Contemporary International Relations* 12 (2015): 1–3; Xinchun Niu, 'Yīdài yīlù xià de zhōngguó zhōngdōng zhànlüè' ('China's Middle East strategy within the framework of the Belt and Road Initiative'), *Foreign Affairs Review* 34, no. 4 (2017): 32–58.

[76] Zhang Chuachu and Chaowei Xiao, 'Bridging the Gap between Overseas and Chinese Perceptions on Sino-Middle Eastern Relations: A Chinese Perspective', *Globalizations* 18, no. 2 (2021): 276.

[77] Xian Xiao, 'Gǎigé kāifàng chūqí zhōngguó yǔ zhōngdōng guójiā jīngmào guānxì de fā zhǎn' ('The development of the trade relations between China and Middle Eastern countries in the early stages of the reform and opening-up period'), *Arab World Studies* 5 (2018): 46–59, 119.

[78] Niu's argument is substantiated by the weak relationship between regional instability and possible disruptions to the flow of oil; see Eugene Gholz, and Daryl G. Press. 'Protecting "The Prize": Oil and the U.S. National Interest', *Security Studies* 19, no. 3 (31 August 2010): 453–485.

[79] Kai Qi, 'Zhōngguó duì yīlākè shíyóu tóuzī de fēngxiǎn fēnxī' ('Risk analysis of Chinese investment in Iraqi oil'), *Arab World Studies*, no. 3 (2017): 86–103, 120.

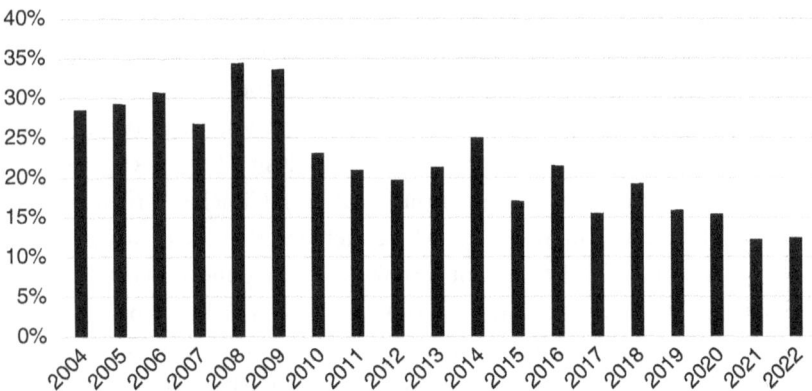

Figure 2 Relative value of the West Asian and North African markets for Chinese engineering and construction companies.

Note: The countries included as part of the Middle East and North Africa are: Algeria, Bahrain, Egypt, Iran, Iraq, Israel, Jordan, Lebanon, Libya, Kuwait, Mauritania, Morocco, Oman, Palestine, Qatar, Saudi Arabia, South Sudan, Sudan, Syria, Tunisia, Türkiye, the UAE, and Yemen. Hong Kong, Taiwan, and Macau are not included in the overall total of the value of the contracts signed by Chinese companies overseas.

Source: Compiled by the authors using data from the National Bureau of Statistics of China.

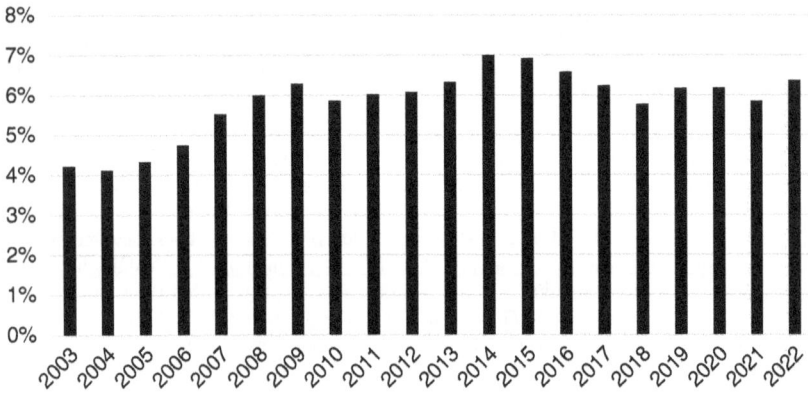

Figure 3 Percentage of Chinese exports to the Middle East and North Africa.

Note: The countries included as part of the Middle East and North Africa are: Algeria, Bahrain, Egypt, Iran, Iraq, Israel, Jordan, Lebanon, Libya, Kuwait, Mauritania, Morocco, Oman, Palestine, Qatar, Saudi Arabia, South Sudan, Sudan, Syria, Tunisia, Türkiye, the UAE, and Yemen. Hong Kong, Taiwan, and Macau are not included in the overall total of the value of the contracts signed by Chinese companies overseas.

Source: Compiled by the authors using data from the International Trade Centre.

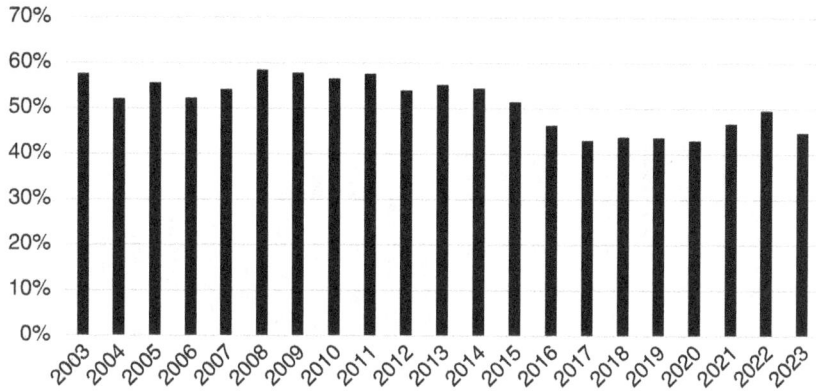

Figure 4 Percentage of Chinese energy imports from the Middle East and North Africa.

Note: The percentages are calculated using the value of Chinese imports of goods whose HS codes are 2709 and 2711. The value of Chinese imports of Iranian energy products is likely to be lower than the real ones. See: Shirzad Azad, 'Bargain and Barter: China's Oil Trade with Iran', *Middle East Policy* 30.1 (2023): 23–35.

Source: Compiled by the authors using data from the International Trade Centre.

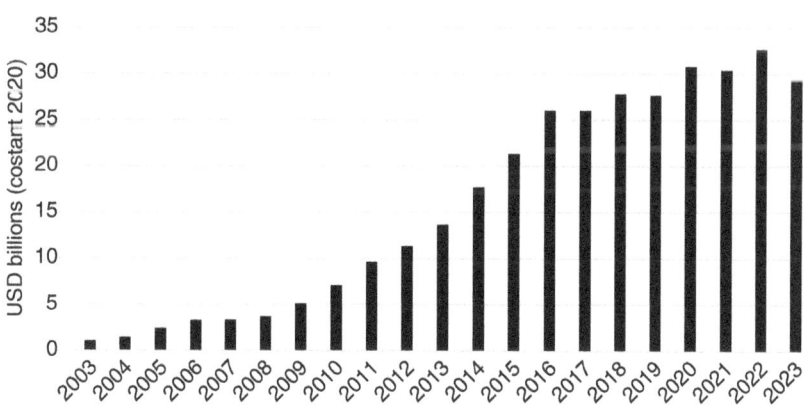

Figure 5 Value of Chinese foreign direct investment (stock) in West Asia and North Africa.

Note: The countries included as part of the Middle East and North Africa are: Algeria, Bahrain, Egypt, Iran, Iraq, Israel, Jordan, Lebanon, Libya, Kuwait, Mauritania, Morocco, Oman, Palestine, Qatar, Saudi Arabia, South Sudan, Sudan, Syria, Tunisia, Türkiye, the UAE, and Yemen.

Source: Compiled by the authors using data from the Chinese Ministry of Commerce, China National Bureau of Statistics, and the State Administration of Foreign Exchange.

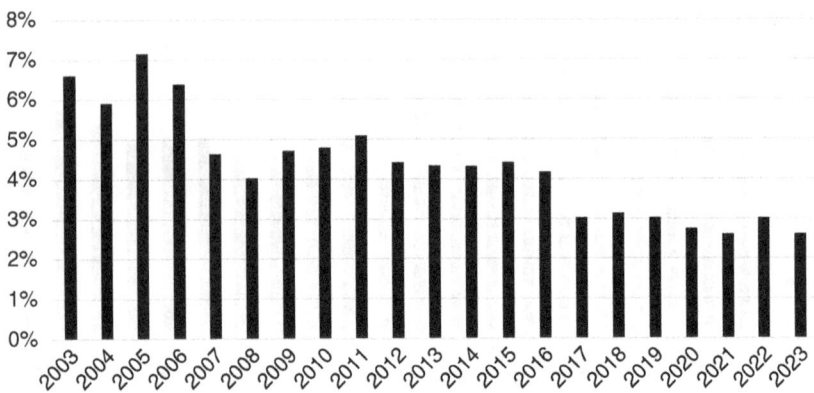

Figure 6 Percentage of Chinese foreign direct investment (stock) in the Middle East and North Africa.

Note: The countries included as part of the Middle East and North Africa are: Algeria, Bahrain, Egypt, Iran, Iraq, Israel, Jordan, Lebanon, Libya, Kuwait, Mauritania, Morocco, Oman, Palestine, Qatar, Saudi Arabia, South Sudan, Sudan, Syria, Tunisia, Türkiye, the UAE, and Yemen. Hong Kong, Taiwan, and Macau are not included in the as part of the overall total of the value of Chinese foreign direct investment overseas.

Source: Compiled by the authors using data from the Chinese Ministry of Commerce, the China National Bureau of Statistics, and the State Administration of Foreign Exchange.

Autonomous Region (XUAR), or the impact arising from the downfall of an ostensibly friendly government (and the full ramifications of the overthrow of the Assadist regime are not yet clear), cannot be ignored and could imperil certain interests in the region, but none of these have constituted a tangible threat to the PRC territorial integrity, or its political regime, and are unlikely to become so anytime soon.[80]

What has enhanced the Middle East's salience in the calculations of Chinese foreign policy elites is the deterioration in Sino-American relations

---

[80] The high tide and subsequent decline of both Dā'ish and al-Nusrah in the Levant during the mid 2010s testify to this point, as there were no spillovers or attacks, perhaps because it also coincided with the heightened securitisation drives in XUAR. It of course remains to be seen how the China-focused aspirations Uyghur militant elements will be dealt with by the new authorities in Syria, which has so far appointed some of them to the Ministry of Defence and is gauging the possibility of granting them citizenship; see Timour Azhari, Khalil Ashawi and Suleiman Al-Khalidi, 'Syria Appoints Some Foreign Islamist Fighters to Its Military, Sources Say', *Reuters*, 31 December 2024, https://short-link.me/14jxq. It should be noted, moreover, that violence against Chinese investment interests has been mainly concentrated in Central Asia so far; see Philip Potter and Chen Wang, *Zero Tolerance: Repression and Political Violence on China's New Silk Road* (Cambridge University Press, 2022).

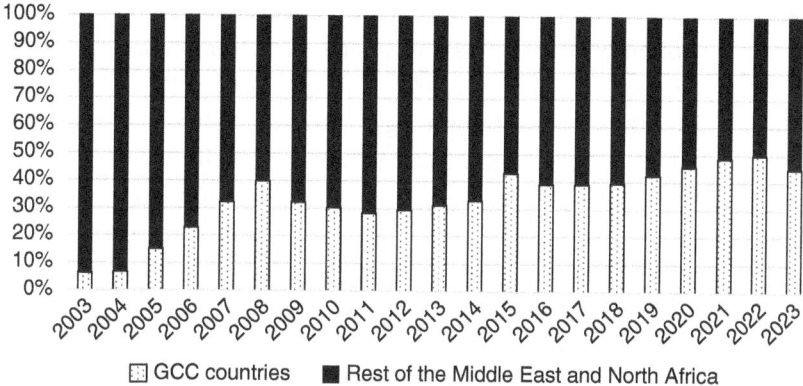

Figure 7 Distribution of Chinese foreign direct investment (stock) in the Middle East and North Africa.

Note: The countries included as part of the Middle East and North Africa are: Algeria, Bahrain, Egypt, Iran, Iraq, Israel, Jordan, Lebanon, Libya, Kuwait, Mauritania, Morocco, Oman, Palestine, Qatar, Saudi Arabia, South Sudan, Sudan, Syria, Tunisia, Türkiye, the UAE, and Yemen. Hong Kong, Taiwan, and Macau are not included in the as part of the overall total of the value of Chinese foreign direct investment overseas.

Source: Compiled by the authors using data from the Chinese Ministry of Commerce, the China National Bureau of Statistics, and the State Administration of Foreign Exchange.

in the mid 2010s, with different takeaways or prescriptions emerging as a result. Some, like Gao Zugui, a researcher at the Central Party School, have argued that the regional turmoil presents opportunities to cooperate and improve relations with the US at a time when security trends in Asia have generated mounting frictions between the two countries.[81] The Chinese push in support of the JCPOA negotiations is a demonstrative example of this dynamic.[82] The region is thus viewed by some as a potential platform for stabilising the Sino-American relationship.

Niu Xinchun and others, such as Liu Zhongmin, another prominent scholar on the Middle East, do not agree with this point of view, arguing that the US has no interest in building long-term cooperation with the PRC in the Middle East, and that American actions in the region do undermine

---

[81] Zugui Gao, 'Zhōngdōng jùbiàn yǐlái zhōngguó yǔ zhōngdōng guójiā de guānxì' ('China–Middle East relations since the great change in the Middle East'), *Arab World Studies* 5 (2015): 14–22.

[82] John W. Garver, 'China and the Iran Nuclear Negotiations: Beijing's Mediation Effort', in James Reardon-Anderson (ed.), *The Red Star and the Crescent: China and the Middle East* (Oxford University Press, 2018), 123–148.

Chinese long-term interests there.⁸³ The 2011 NATO bombing campaign in Libya is often brought up as an example of this, leading as it did to the hasty evacuation of over 36,000 citizens from the PRC.⁸⁴ Likewise, some consider the violence embroiling the XUAR to be a by-product of the American invasions that weakened state authority in Afghanistan and Iraq, allowing in turn all types of transnational networks and groups to operate and grow in strength.⁸⁵ They point, moreover, to the recent US campaigns to limit Sino-Middle Eastern economic and technological cooperation: as Niu summarised in a short commentary in early 2023, 'the US and China worry about the Middle East becoming a card in the other's hand, forming a typical security dilemma'.⁸⁶

What emerges from the discussions of Chinese foreign policy elites is a complex picture, and one in which the importance of the region is increasingly acknowledged. Although the PRC's survival or the so-called 'core interests' (héxīn lìyì) are not at risk, there are many 'normal' interests that might be suddenly threatened and damaged.⁸⁷ The intensifying competition with the US has made reluctant Chinese foreign policy elites more sensitive to that eventuality. The Middle East is therefore increasingly relevant in their eyes as a consequence of great power rivalry, but only up to a point.

Searching for the Right Approach

When considering much of the 2010–2023 debates among Chinese foreign policy elites concerning the regional order, it is worth recalling that the PRC's diplomatic and security interactions with local state actors have evolved and deepened in tandem. Building upon institutions and processes that had been initiated in the early 2000s, the PRC has utilised a variety of diplomatic fora, such as the China-Arab States Cooperation Forum,

---

83 'Niu, 'Zhōngguó yǔ zhōngdōng'; Liu, 'Zhōngdōng biànjú yǔ shìjiè zhǔyào dàguó zhōngdōng zhànlüè de tiáozhěng' ('The Middle East upheaval and the readjustment of great powers' Middle East strategies'), *West Asia and North Africa* 2 (2012): 4–22.
84 Ghiselli, *Protecting China's Interests Overseas*, 114–143.
85 For example, see Lirong Ma, 'Shè jiāng bào kǒng shíjiàn zhōng de "zhōngdōng yīnsù" yǔ guójì fǎnkǒng hézuò' ('The "Middle East factor" in terrorism in Xinjiang and international anti-terrorism cooperation'), *Arab World Studies* 1 (2015): 23–37.
86 Xinchun Niu, 'Měiguó zài zhōngdōng dānxīn zhōngguó shénme?' ('What does the United States worry about China in the Middle East?'), *Aisixiang*, 2 February 2023, www.aisixiang.com/data/140436.html.
87 The PRC's 'core interests' are usually understood to comprise six components: state sovereignty, national security, territorial integrity, national reunification, the constitutional political system and overall social stability, and basic safeguards for ensuring sustainable economic and social development.

the Forum on China-Africa Cooperation, and, to a limited extent, the Shanghai Cooperation Organisation, to strengthen its relations with its regional counterparts; it also appointed special envoys to address hotspot issues across the greater Middle East, and has facilitated the brokerage of the Saudi–Iranian détente in 2023, among others.[88] Its participation in peacekeeping initiatives, such as the United Nations Interim Force in Lebanon, antipiracy operations in the Gulf of Aden (from late 2008), as well as the opening of the military base in Djibouti, have helped the PRC add a military dimension to its presence in the region.[89]

By the mid 2010s, however, Chinese foreign policy elites were expressing doubts about whether their country's approach to the Middle East, marked by the diplomatic and security forays set out earlier, was sufficient and up to the task of tackling the various regional challenges there. Hua Liming, for example, bluntly argued that the PRC's Middle East policy had to be rethought:

> In the new century, China must define its strategic interests and goals in the Middle East. This is to gain greater influence in the Middle East and truly become a responsible power for peace and stability, thereby ensuring China's energy security, the tranquillity of its western frontier, and reducing strategic pressure in the East and South China Seas. To this end, China should reposition the Middle East in its diplomacy and not spare diplomatic resources to make a difference ... When we discuss China's Middle East strategy, there is one issue that cannot be avoided. This is the relationship between the policy of burying its head in the sand and being a responsible world power. A responsible world power is one that has to take responsibility. If it does not, it has no voice in regional affairs. In the Middle East, it would be detrimental for China itself to continue to stay aloof.[90]

Hua was not the only one to write that Beijing was 'burying its head in the sand', as it were. Niu Xinchun, described the current policy approach as 'doing nothing [in the Middle East], reacting to something [at the UN]', though he praised the fact that the PRC had become more active in promoting and hosting peace talks.[91] Certainly, not everyone agrees. Some have lauded the current Chinese approach, embodying Xi Jinping's 'great power diplomacy' (*dàguó wàijiāo*), a concept unveiled

---

[88] For a comprehensive description, see Murphy, *China's Rise in the Global South*, 55–95.
[89] For a comprehensive description, see Ghiselli, *Protecting China's Interests Overseas*, 203–240.
[90] Hua, 'Duì dāngqián zhōngdōng júshì de jǐ diǎn kànfǎ'.
[91] Niu, 'Yīdài yīlù xià de zhōngguó zhōngdōng zhànlüè', 42–43.

at the Eighteenth Party Congress in 2012, as being more than enough.[92] While acknowledging that there were challenges that had to be overcome, Sun Degang, a prominent expert based at Fudan University, has written a number of articles highlighting the newly found proactiveness of the PRC's 'partnership diplomacy' (*huǒbàn wàijiāo*), the exchanges carried out by the International Liaison Department of the Chinese Communist Party with Middle Eastern political parties, as well as the development of a new 'soft military presence' (*róuxìng jūnshì cúnzài*) in the region.[93] In other words, foreign policy was re-calibrating in a way that constituted an appropriate response to the regional situation.

One reason as to why foreign policy elites have interpreted the PRC's regional approach in different ways – as insufficient (i.e., needing to assume responsibility) or appropriate (i.e., doing enough through existing 'great power diplomacy') – is that there are divergent views among them over what exactly drives Chinese entanglements in the Middle East. Tian Wenlin, a researcher at CICIR, stated that Chinese experts often misinterpret the dynamics propelling Sino-Middle Eastern relations.[94] Though many believe that Chinese initiatives, such as the four-point proposal regarding the Palestine–Israel conflict, and actions, like its stance at the UNSC, have played a crucial role in eliciting regional engagement with the PRC, Tian sees endogenous developments in the Middle East as being far more relevant. In other words, Chinese influence has only increased because there is local appetite for what the PRC has to offer, rather than because it has succeeded in making itself more attractive. Even in the case of Iran, a country that is viewed as one of the PRC's closest partners in the region, some have repeatedly warned that policymakers should not believe that Chinese diplomatic and economic influence there

---

[92] Meng Wang, 'Yīdài yīlù' shì yù xià de zhōngguó zhōngdōng wàijiāo: Chuánchéng yǔ dāndāng' ('China's Middle East diplomacy within the framework of the Belt and Road Initiative: legacy and responsibilities'), *West Asia and Africa* 4 (2018): 21–41; Bo Wang and Quan Yao, 'Xīn shíqí zhōngguó zhōngdōng wàijiāo sīxiǎng gòujiàn yánjiū' ('Research on the development of China's Middle East diplomatic thinking in the new era'), *Arab World Studies* 2 (2019): 76–90, 119–120.

[93] Degang Sun, 'Lùn 21 shìjì zhōngguó duì: Zhōngdōng guójiā de huǒbàn wàijiāo' ('Discussing China's partnership diplomacy toward Middle East countries in the Twenty-First Century'), *World Economy and Politics* 7 (2019): 106–130, 158–159; Degang Sun and Tongyu Wu, 'Lùn zhōngguó duì ālābó guójiā de zhèngdǎng wàijiāo' ('Discussing China's party diplomacy toward Arab countries'), *Arab World Studies* 4 (2021): 3–24, 157; Degang Sun and Shuai Zhang, 'Gǎigé kāifàng yǐlái zhōngguó cānyù liánhéguó: Zài zhōngdōng wéihé xíngdòng de lǐniàn yǔ shíjiàn' ('Concepts and practice of China's participation in peacekeeping operations in the Middle East since the reform and opening-up period'), *Arab World Studies* 5 (2018): 14–28, 118–119.

[94] Wenlin Tian, 'Yīdài yīlù: Yǔ zhōngguó de zhōngdōng zhànlüè' ('The Belt and Road Initiative and China's Middle East strategy'), *West Asia and Africa* 2 (2016): 127–145.

would remain the same following the potential end of American-imposed sanctions.[95]

Li Weijian has likewise argued that Chinese initiatives, especially those outside the fields of trade and investment, often fail to gain traction in the region.[96] The PRC can offer much needed economic support and a developmental experience different from that of the West, but, as Li notes, the pursuit of security dominates Middle Eastern politics, and local state actors do not see the usefulness of forums and conferences led or proposed by the PRC. Moreover, Chinese proactivity has sometimes had negative reactions. That was the case when the PRC, together with Russia, cast a series of vetoes at the UNSC between 2011 and 2012 in defence of the Assadist regime in Syria. As a result, China's special envoy for the Middle East, Ambassador Wu Sike, had to tour the GCC member-states to explain that Beijing was protecting the principle of sovereignty in the face of Western pressure, rather than acting specifically in favour of Bashar al-Assad.[97] Relatedly, Chinese scholars are acutely aware that the PRC stance on Syria was not positively received by Middle Eastern audiences.[98]

In weighing the future of Sino-Middle East relations, some Chinese foreign policy elites have wondered whether the current status quo, in conjunction with the prevailing conservative approach, is sustainable. Niu Xinchun has argued, in an implicit warning, that it is extremely unlikely that warm diplomatic relations between the PRC and the region could be sustained without stronger and deeper economic ties.[99] Echoing this view somewhat, Zhang Chuchu claims that instability and economic backwardness have prevented the implementation of the vast majority of the highly publicised BRI agreements.[100] The PRC's own economic slowdown as part of its 'new normal' (*xīn chángtài*), that is, the decline in economic growth, might create additional problems. These various issues were more or less implicitly recognised by most of the authors of the articles surveyed

---

[95] Hongda Fan, 'Zhōngguó zài yīlǎng tuījìn yīdài yīlù_zhànlüè chàngyì de zhèngzhì huánjìng yǔ yīnyìng' ('The political environment and reaction to China's promotion of the Belt and Road Initiative in Iran'), *West Asia and Africa* 2 (2016): 49–64.
[96] Weijian Li, 'Zhōngguó zài zhōngdōng: Huàyǔ yǔ xiànshí' ('China in the Middle East: rhetoric and practice'), *West Asia and Africa* 5 (2017): 3–19.
[97] Ruyi Li and Feng Hu, 'Wú sīkē: Hànwèi zhèngyì, zhōngguó céng liánxù sāncì dòngyòng ānlǐhuì fǒujué quán' ('Wu Sike: protecting justice, China uses the veto three times at the UNSC'), *Beijing Daily*, 21 September 2019, https://short-link.me/14jxR.
[98] Zhenhua Li, 'Ālābó wǎngluò yúqíng fēn xī' ('Analysis of Arab online public opinion'), *Arab World Studies* 3 (2013): 107–120.
[99] Niu, 'Yīdài yīlù xià de zhōngguó zhōngdōng zhànlüè'.
[100] Chuchu Zhang, 'Yī shí zhèngmíng: Zhōngguó yǔ zhōngdōng guójiā de jīchǔ shèshī hézuò' ('Dispelling the myth: the cooperation between China and Middle Eastern countries in the construction of basic infrastructure'), *West Asia and Africa* 4 (2021): 54–73, 157–158.

in our analysis, suggesting that an economy-centric reading of the PRC's presence in the Middle East remains well-entrenched and pervasive.

Against this background, different perspectives have developed about how Chinese foreign policy should interact with the Middle East.[101] The most radical position, though seemingly the minority one, is that the PRC should embrace great power competition with the US and make it the main driver of its regional approach, significantly elevating the strategic importance of this theatre in relation to its national interests. To some extent, Niu Xinchun argues, this would mean reproducing the PRC's Middle East strategies during the Maoist era, when there were many instances of overt political and military involvement.[102] The vast majority of foreign policy experts, however, clearly advocate for continuity and keeping to the current course. Though the latter might also call for paying more attention to US moves and seizing opportunities to undermine them, such as when Iran and the other members of the so-called axis of resistance undermine American actions,[103] they insist that the PRC should not take sides in favour of any regional or extra-regional powers. To varying degrees, they oppose any and all military commitments, including outright embeddedness in the security architecture (in terms of alliances or security provisions) as the costs and risks would be far higher than any real gain that would arise from these. While recognising some of the limits to this approach, Sun Degang writes that 'China's global partnership network is built on the basis of "partnerships, not alliances", and seeking common ground while reserving differences. This is in line with China's diplomatic philosophy and the interests of all parties.'[104]

Throughout our analysis of the Chinese sources, we could not find any clear statement advocating outright PRC alignment with any specific local state actor to the detriment of others. Hua Liming, who was quoted calling for the PRC to assume responsibility in the Middle East, warned not only against taking sides but also that any policies aimed at 'squeezing traditional American power' should be avoided.[105] This stance likely originates from an awareness, as noted by Niu in the case of Syria, that regional

---

[101] Xinchun Niu, 'Yǔ měiguó gòngchǔ: Zhōngguó zhōngdōng zhèngcè de xīn tiǎozhàn' ('Coexistence with the United States: the new challenge for China's Middle East policy'), *Contemporary International Relations* 11 (2022): 9–16, 24.
[102] Ibid.
[103] Ruiheng Li, 'Zhōngdōng "dǐkàng zhóu xīn" de xīngqǐ jí qiánjǐng' ('The rise of the "Axis of Resistance" in the Middle East and its prospects'), *Contemporary International Relations* 4 (2024): 60–76.
[104] Sun, 'Lùn 21 shìjì zhōngguó duì', 128–129.
[105] Hua, 'Duì dāngqián zhōngdōng júshì de jǐ diǎn kànfǎ'.

stability cannot be achieved 'without the support of the international community, including the US and the European countries'.[106] Instead, what foreign policy elites endorse is for the PRC to leverage its economic power to promote a 'development first' agenda, pushing local leaders to focus on economic growth, rather than expending resources on pointless regional rivalries and conflicts.[107] Supporting industrialisation, as well as cross-regional integration, are the key pillars of this approach.[108]

The logic behind it is that by pursuing development, the Middle East would stabilise into a prosperous and well-governed space, limiting in turn the influence of other extra-regional great powers such as the US and Russia as local courtship for their support recedes – a win-win scenario for the PRC. More optimistically, local state actors, now economically intertwined with each other (and the PRC), would make the appropriate efforts together to create a new Middle Eastern security mechanism (and along with it, a regional order) owned and managed by themselves. This would allow the PRC in turn to maximise its interests in the region while maintaining cordial relations with all parties without any major security commitments on its part at any point in the future. This vision is tied to the expectation that the Middle East is already showing signs that it is headed in that direction, as epitomised for instance by the Saudi–Iranian détente, the (then ongoing) re-integration of Assadist Syria, and Arab–Israeli normalisation under the Abraham Accords, among others. As we discuss in the Conclusion, there are already some analyses of the conflict in Gaza that started in late 2023 suggesting that Chinese foreign policy elites feel vindicated by the soundness of this assessment.

It is important to emphasise that the articulation of an alternative, more assertive approach towards the Middle East is probably complicated by the nature of the PRC's own policymaking processes. Some analysts have pointed out that insufficient coordination among the many domestic institutions that manage Chinese activities in the region has often transformed correct strategic choices into implementation failures, irritating regional

---

[106] Jiabao Li, 'Měiguó zài xùlìyǎ bèi biānyuán huàle?' ('Has the United States been side-lined in Syria?'), *People's Daily*, 19 February 2019, http://world.people.com.cn/n1/2019/0219/c1002-30805257.html.

[107] Guigui Xi and Shuisheng Chen, '"Yīdài yīlù" bèijǐng xià zhōngguó de zhōngdōng jīngjì wàijiāo' ('China's economic diplomacy in the Middle East within the framework of the Belt and Road Initiative'), *Arab World Studies* 6 (2016): 48–59, 117.

[108] Min Wei, 'Zhōngguó yǔ zhōngdōng guójì chǎnnéng hézuò de lǐlùn yǔ zhèngcè fēnxī' ('Theory and policy analysis of Sino-Middle Eastern production cooperation'), *Arab World Studies* 6 (2016): 3–20, 116.

partners or causing serious economic losses for the PRC.[109] Tensions in East Asia involving the US likewise limit the 'diplomatic resources' (*wàijiāo zīyuán*) that the country can allocate elsewhere, including the Middle East, to protect its interests.[110] Beyond that, many scholars also agree that there is not enough expertise about the region within the PRC, contributing at times to the production of shallow knowledge about the Middle East and its problems.

On the Chinese Vision

In this section, we have shed light on how Chinese foreign policy elites have understood the evolution of the situation in the Middle East over the past decade, as well as their evaluations of the PRC's interests and approaches there. While the regional situation is uncertain and turbulent, they perceive a new order coming into being: local state actors are recalibrating their domestic and foreign policies towards regional integration and resolving their conflicts as the US undergoes 'strategic contraction'. However, this outcome needs time to mature. In terms of their country's interests in the Middle East, they appraise them to be normal on a global scale, though gaining some significance due to Sino-American competition. While a minority are calling for adjustments in the PRC's approach to the region, the majority abjure any shifts in the political or security domains beyond what has already been accomplished by 'great power diplomacy'. They all do, however, envision the PRC playing an important economic role as positive trends in the region become manifest. Based on this snapshot of the discussions among Chinese foreign policy elites, a major transformation in Chinese foreign policy in the Middle East over the short or mid-term is a highly unlikely prospect.

Saudi Arabia: Forging a New Regional Order

This section examines how the changes in the Middle East regional order, and the PRC's place within it as an extra-regional great power, were perceived by Saudi foreign policy elites. A key feature in their assessment

---

[109] Meng Wang, 'Lùn "yīdài yīlù" chàngyì zài zhōngdōng de shíshī' ('Discussing the implementation of the Belt and Road in the Middle East'), *Contemporary International Relations* 3 (2017): 16–22, 36; Xinchun Niu, 'Xiǎngxiàng yǔ zhēnxiàng: Zhōngguó de zhōngdōng zhèngcè' ('Imagination and reality: China's Middle East policy'), *West Asia and Africa* 4 (2021): 25–53, 156–157.

[110] Wentao Li, 'Zhōng fēi jūnshì ānquán hézuò xiàng shēn céngcì màijìn' ('China–Africa military security cooperation is moving to a deeper level'), *World Affairs* 15 (2018): 58–59.

of the region was that it was marred by a deep crisis caused by external subversion, primarily originating from Iran, and internal failures in governance and development. Amidst this turbulence, amplified by perceptions of American withdrawal from the region, they increasingly identified an opportunity for Saudi Arabia to assume a leading Arab role, filling a 'strategic vacuum' (*farāgh istrātījī*) in the Middle East arising from the collective weakness of Arab states in the face of expansionary projects from hostile regional actors. This potential Saudi role was believed to assume greater salience (and tenability) as more progress was made through domestic reform under Vision 2030, the Saudi roadmap for national rejuvenation that has become a fixture of foreign policy elite discourse since it was launched in 2016, bestowing the state with new resources and power projection capabilities.[111] The 2010s was thus viewed by Saudi foreign policy elites as a transformative, albeit fraught, moment for the Kingdom's place vis-à-vis the regional order.

During this same period, Sino-Saudi ties were increasingly cast in terms of aiding in the obtaining of the Saudi state's developmental and multilateralisation goals and thus facilitating this domestic and regional turning point. The PRC's economic and technological strengths render it a key partner for achieving the modernisation objectives of the Saudi state and, on a larger regional scale, the potential to stabilise, through the power of integrative projects such as the BRI, the whole of the Middle East. Its ascension, in conjunction with other non-Western actors, offers strategic options for the Saudi leadership, and enables the latter to negotiate more favourable arrangements with the US or extract concessions from it. This explains the penchant in the discourse to critically (and positively) contrast Sino-Saudi bilateral relations with the equivalent relationship with the US.

At the same time, there is little evidence from the discourse of Saudi foreign policy elites that Chinese involvement in the regional security architecture was countenanced as a serious scenario, at least over the short and medium terms. Rather, many of these elites continually stressed that the US remained their principal security partner, and that there was no Eastward re-alignment in the country's foreign policy, but a general trend towards multilateralisation and strategic hedging. Thus, while the PRC was, and remains, celebrated as a great power in Saudi foreign policy discourse, and as one that exerts positive influence on the Kingdom and the regional order, it is confined within economic parameters.

---

[111] Vision 2030 is the national transformation plan unveiled by Crown Mohammed bin Salman in 2016. For more information via a Saudi state source, see www.vision2030.gov.sa/en.

The Twin Sources of Regional Turbulence

Over the past decade, Saudi foreign policy elites have articulated a relatively consistent diagnosis of what they consider to be the major causes of instability in the Middle East, identifying two primary catalysts for regional disorder. The first, as touched upon in one of the earliest interviews given by Crown Prince Mohammed bin Salman, is the danger posed by a collection of ideologically driven actors that instrumentalise violent and subversive propaganda to undermine the integrity and cohesion of Arab governments and societies.[112] These encompass political and militant non-state organisations such as the Muslim Brotherhood, al-Qaeda in the Arabian Peninsula, ISIL, Hizbollah in Lebanon, and the Houthīs in Yemen, to major states such as Qatar, Türkiye, and the Islamic Republic of Iran. Among these, the latter is construed, as 'Adel al-Jubeir, the Saudi Foreign Minister for 2015–2018 put it, as 'the big[gest] menace' by far.[113]

From the early 2010s, negative perceptions of Iran were widely entrenched in popular and elite discourses, not only in Saudi Arabia, but across much of the Arab world.[114] For many onlookers based within the Kingdom and beyond, Iran appeared, throughout the evolving events of the Arab Spring and in its intervention to support the Baʿathist regime in Syria, as an aggressive power which occupied 'four Arab capitals' and which aspired to control even more through the sectarian sub-state proxies it had created.[115] The Director of the Gulf Research Centre and prominent geopolitical commentator ʿAbdulaziz bin Sager described Iran as a

---

[112] 'Liqa al-amir Mohammed bin Salman kamilan' ('The full interview with Prince Muhammad bin Salman') AlArabiya (YouTube), 3 May 2017, www.youtube.com/watch?v=AZXSa6WZ-dA.

[113] 'Muqabala khassa / 'adel al-jubeir – wazir ad-dawla lil shuun al-kharijiyya al-su'udiyya' ('Special interview / 'Adel al-Jubeir – Minister of State for Saudi Foreign Affairs') AlArabiya (YouTube), 23 September 2019, www.youtube.com/watch?v=rIJhzwwCh_c.

[114] Several surveys conducted from 2011 onwards show sizable majorities in many sampled Arab states expressing negative views of Iran, see James Zogby, 'Arab Attitudes toward Iran, 2011', Arab American Institute Foundation, 2011; Shibley Telhami, 'Annual Arab Public Opinion Survey', University of Maryland, 2011; Mehran Kamrava and Hamideh Dorzadeh, 'Arab Opinion Toward Iran 2019/2020', Doha Institute, 22 December 2020, https://short-link.me/10d43.

[115] The comment on the Islamic Republic controlling 'four Arab capitals' is attributed to Heydar Moslehi, the former minister of intelligence (2009–2013) during Mahmoud Ahmadinejad's administration. The phrase entered into wide use in the Saudi and Arab press and came to symbolise Iran's unbridled ambitions in the Middle East; see 'Wazir Irani sabiq: nusaytir 'ala arba' 'awasim 'arabiyya' ('Former Iranian minister: we control four Arab capitals') AlArabiya, 2 April 2015, https://short-link.me/10d3Q.

hegemony-seeking actor in the Middle East – a near-consensus view in the discourse.[116]

The prioritisation of the Iranian threat among Saudi foreign policy elites is also clear. Statements from the Saudi Council of Ministers, as well as the Crown Prince, recurrently contained condemnations that depicted the Kingdom as the main target of the Islamic Republic and its allies.[117] In one instance, they proclaimed Iran to be violating 'the foundational basis of international law and the principles of good neighbourliness … and [thus constituting] an extreme danger to regional and global security and peace'.[118] Prince Turki al-Faisal, the former head of the General Intelligence Directorate (1979–2001) and current chairman of the King Faisal Centre for Research and Islamic Studies (KFCRIS), identified Iranian expansionism as a core danger to Saudi national security.[119]

What exacerbated this danger from Iran, in the eyes of Saudi foreign policy elites, was the extreme ideological beliefs attributed to its leadership. The Crown Prince, for example, publicly questioned in 2017 the possibility of reaching an accommodation with 'a regime … whose constitution mandates asserting control over the Muslim world and spreading Twelver Shi'ism'.[120] Al-Jubeir similarly argued that Iran was led by a regime that had an intransigent 'desire to export the revolution' and displayed little respect for a Westphalian regional order in the Middle East.[121] Several

---

[116] 'Atawatur al-su'udi al-irani ma' Abdulaziz bin sagr | podcast fijan, idtha'at thamaniyya' ('Saudi–Iranian tensions with Abdulaziz bin Sagr') (YouTube), 10 November 2021, www.youtube.com/watch?v=YvjaL6L1UTo.

[117] 'Khadim al-Haramayyin al-Sharifayyin yaras jalsat majlis al-wuzara' ('The custodian of the two holy mosques oversees the ministerial council'), Saudi Press Agency, 16 January 2018, https://sp.spa.gov.sa/viewfullstory.php?lang=ar&newsid=1710353; 'Khadim al-Haramayyin al-Sharifayyin yaras jalsat majlis al-wuzara' ('The custodian of the two holy mosques oversees the ministerial council'), Saudi Press Agency, 25 February 2020, https://sp.spa.gov.sa/viewfullstory.php?newsid=2039087; Salman al-Dawsari, 'Ma ba'd 'idwan iran al-'askari' ('What happens after Iran's military aggression'), Asharq al-Awsat, 10 November 2017, https://short-link.me/14jyA.

[118] 'Khadim al-Haramayyin al-Sharifayyin yaras jalsat majlis al-wuzara iqafat uwla' ('The custodian of the two holy mosques oversees the ministerial council'), Saudi Press Agency, 11 January 2016, https://sp.spa.gov.sa/viewfullstory.php?lang=ar&newsid=1444854.

[119] 'Keynote Address by HRH Prince Turki Al Faisal at the 2013 Arab-U.S. Policymakers Conference', National Council on U.S.-Arab Relations (YouTube), 29 October 2013, www.youtube.com/watch?v=gqRJmcDwAA4&t=2s.

[120] 'Liqa al-amir Mohammed bin Salman kamilan' ('The full interview with Prince Muhammad bin Salman') AlArabiya (YouTube), 3 May 2017, www.youtube.com/watch?v=AZXSa6WZ-dA.

[121] 'Muqabala khassa / 'Adel al-Jubeir – wazir ad-dawla lil shuun al-kharijiya al-su'udiyya' ('Special interview / 'Adel al-Jubeir – Minister of State for Saudi Foreign Affairs'), AlArabiya (YouTube), 20 July 2016, www.youtube.com/watch?v=s94UlM5v6Uc; 'Muhadarat ma'ali al-wazir 'adel al-jubeir fi al-ma'had al-malaki lil 'ilaqat aduwaliya – Chatham House 07/09/2016' ('Lecture of His Excellency Minister 'Adel al-Jubeir in the

Saudi analysts, most notably ʿAbdullah al-Saʿud, currently the head of research at the Ministry of Foreign Affairs, have elaborated on this idea, claiming that the Islamic Republic embraced a vision of the region that aimed to do away with the nation-state in favour of sub-national solidarities predicated upon narrow sectarian conceptions of identity and affiliation.[122]

If the first catalyst causing instability in the Middle East can be thought of as external, the second is more internal in nature, and revolves around the failure of many Arab governments to implement timely political and economic reforms. Prince Turki al-Faisal observed in one of his speeches that many regimes in the region were facing a crisis of governance involving an erosion of the social contracts binding them to their citizens.[123] This neglect, and concomitant decline in overall governance, created an environment ripe for the proliferation of mostly Iranian-abetted, sub-national militias and political organisations seeking to fill the newfound vacuums arising from the withdrawal or collapse of centralised state authorities. In the case of regimes struggling with mounting popular discontent and even rebellion, as in Syria and Iraq, their elites had courted and facilitated Iranian intervention out of self-preservation – all to the detriment of the long-term well-being of their states and societies.

Accordingly, we find that Saudi foreign policy elites see a type of feedback loop at play between these two catalysts behind a dismal and broken regional order: the weakening of Arab states (or 'non-states' (*al-lā dawla*) as one commentator calls them), a by-product of the failures of rulers themselves, paved the way for a diverse of set of ideological actors, crowned by Iran, to set up alternative centres of (sectarian) authority and rule, accelerating in turn the withering away of the (Arab) states and the national communities that underpin them.[124] Mansur Almarzuqi, an academic

---

Royal Academy on international relations'), Ministry of Foreign Affairs of Saudi Arabia (YouTube), 12 September 2016, www.youtube.com/watch?v=8DccYGnizGE.

[122] Abdullah K. Al-Saud and Joseph A. Kéchichian, 'The Evolving Security Landscape Around the Arabian Peninsula: A Saudi Perspective', Istituto Affari Internazionali, 8 June 2020; Abdulmajeed Saud Manqarah, 'Competing Models in the Middle East: Saudi Arabia and Iran', KFCRIS Special Reports, 22 July 2019, http://kfcris.com/en/view/post/220.

[123] 'Keynote Address by HRH Prince Turki Al Faisal at the 2014 Arab-U.S. Policymakers Conference', National Council on U.S.-Arab Relations (YouTube), 30 October 2014, www.youtube.com/watch?v=n5kX0EgAu0k; 'Keynote Address by HRH Prince Turki Al Faisal at the 2015 Arab-U.S. Policymakers Conference', National Council on U.S.-Arab Relations (YouTube), 22 October 2015, www.youtube.com/watch?v=oKkTG-VG6Es.

[124] Majid al-Hujaylan, 'Iran wa al-la dawla al-'arabiyya' ('Iran and the Arab non-state') *Majalat al-Faisal* 477–478 (July–August 2016): 182–183.

at the Prince Saud Al-Faisal Institute for Diplomatic Studies associated with the Ministry of Foreign Affairs, spelled this out by asserting that the Islamic Republic intentionally sought to foment instability in many surrounding states as a way of enhancing the appeal and reach of its sectarian project across much of the Middle East.[125] Likewise, Muhammad al-Sulami, the head of the International Institute for Iranian Studies based in Riyadh, argued that Iran intentionally blocks efforts at re-centralising and strengthening the national government in places such as Lebanon and Iraq in order to safeguard its influence there.[126]

Pathways for Stabilising the Regional Order

These twin sources of regional ailments reveal much with regards to how Saudi foreign policy elites understand the Kingdom's positionality within the Middle East. As they imagine it, Saudi Arabia has long adhered to a pragmatic and sober foreign policy rooted in 'moderation' (*i'tidāl*) that rejects irredentism and interference in the affairs of others, and a vision of development and modernisation that places a premium on stability.[127] This conservatively reformist approach is viewed by many Saudi foreign policy elites, including the influential commentator Ali al-Shihabi, as one possessing an undeniable and proven record of success, standing in stark contrast to the failures of the Kingdom's many adversaries – whether they be the Iranian-backed sectarians of the present or the pan-Arab republicans or revolutionary Marxists of earlier years.[128] The approach approximates in fact the status of a 'model' (*namudhaj*) that offers, they would argue, a tried-and-tested, non-ideological pathway for a turbulent region that had long embraced radical and ultimately futile solutions to its problems, and one that is given further credence by the Kingdom's status as the last remaining major Arab power in the Middle East.[129]

---

[125] Mansur Almarzuqi, 'Al-thabit wal mutahawil fi muhadidat al-siyassa al-kharijiyya al-su'udiyya' ('The constant and changing in the determinants of Saudi foreign policy'), *Rouya Türkiyyah* 4, no. 2 (2015): 123.

[126] Muhammad bin Sagr al-Sulami, 'Mustaqbal al-'ilaqat al-su'udiyya al-iraniyya' ('The future of Saudi–Iranian relations'), *Majalat al-Faisal* 477–478 (July–August 2016): 107–108.

[127] 'Keynote Address by HRH Prince Turki Al Faisal at the 2012 Arab-U.S. Policymakers Conference', National Council on U.S.-Arab Relations (YouTube), 2 November 2012, www.youtube.com/watch?v=DTKKk_xC7uE.

[128] Ali Al-Shihabi, *The Saudi Kingdom: Between the Jihadi Hammer and the Iranian Anvil* (Markus Weiner Publishers, 2016).

[129] 'Muhadarat ma'ali al-wazir 'adel al-jubeir fi al-ma'had al-malaki lil 'ilaqat aduwaliya – Chatham House 07/09/2016'.

With this self-image of Saudi Arabia in mind, how do these foreign policy elites propose tackling the twin catalysts imperilling the region and, by extension, the country's national security? What is, in other words, the Saudi solution to an unstable regional order? With respect to the first dilemma, the basic contours of their thinking on how to address the threat posed by ideological actors has remained relatively consistent for much of the 2010s. As they see it, the most desired and ideal outcome is for the Islamic Republic, and to a lesser extent, similar actors such as Türkiye and Israel, to forsake their regional ambitions and allow for equitable political solutions to emerge in divided polities such as Lebanon, Iraq, Yemen, and Libya.[130]

Yet convincing Iran to act as a Westphalian nation-state willing to respect international law is easier said than done. Negotiations with the Iranian leadership, which is sometimes described as 'deceitful' and 'malevolent', have been frustrating, and especially so in light of the Islamic Republic's alleged track record of reneging on past understandings and agreements.[131] As al-Jubeir declared in one talk, 'engagement with Iran does not work, we tried for the last forty years'.[132] Salman al-Dowsari, the editor-in-chief of *Asharq al-Awsat* for 2014–2016 and current minister of media, echoed many when he stated that the notion that there were dovish reformists among Iranian elite which one could reach an accord with was a laughable one, declaring that talks with Iran were simply unrealistic.[133]

It should be noted that despite the severe deterioration in relations post-2016, negotiations were never off the table: Saudi leaders repeatedly signalled, notwithstanding deep mistrust towards their counterparts, that geography and a shared religious and civilisational tradition dictated the need to reach an amicable solution with the Islamic Republic.[134] Prominent

---

[130] Salman al-Dawsari, 'Turkiyya wa istinsakh al-milishiyyat al-iraniyya' ('Türkiye and the copying of the Iranian militia (model)') *Asharq al-Awsat*, 9 February 2020, https://short-link.me/10d4v.

[131] Al-Dawsari, 'Turkiyya wa istinsakh al-milishiyyat al-iraniyya'.

[132] 'Davos 2017 – A Conversation with Adel Al Jubeir on Middle East Security', World Economic Forum (YouTube), 21 January 2017, www.youtube.com/watch?v=FocrKQ9ZDTc.

[133] Tariq al-Hamid, 'Hal fi al-su'udiyya suqur wa hamaim?' ('Are there hawks and doves in Saudi Arabia?'), *Asharq al-Awsat*, 27 July 2015; Salman al-Dawsari, 'Al-hiwar ma' Iran fikra ghayir waqi'iyya' ('Dialogue with Iran is an unrealistic idea'), *Asharq al-Awsat*, 6 January 2017, https://short-link.me/14jAh.

[134] 'Muqabala khassa / 'adel al-jubeir – wazir ad-dawla lil shuun al-kharijiyya al-su'udiyya' ('Special interview / 'Adel al-Jubeir – Minister of State for Saudi Foreign Affairs'), AlArabiya (YouTube), 23 September 2019, www.youtube.com/watch?v=rIJhzwwCh_c; 'Keynote Address by Prince Turki Al Faisal (2019 Arab-US Policymakers Conference)', National Council on U.S.-Arab Relations (YouTube), 1 November 2019, www.youtube.com/watch?v=6-SPY7PCJ_s&t=679s.

observers of Saudi–Iranian relations, such as 'Awad al-Badi, an academic at KFCRIS and advisor to Prince Turki al-Faisal, has long expressed the need for such a dialogue.[135] Bin Sager has similarly advocated for this position, stating in an article published in the *New York Times* jointly written with Hossein Mousavian, a former Iranian official and diplomat, that there is an imperative need for both sides to de-escalate and talk.[136]

Though negotiations were clearly considered to be a difficult endeavour blemished by mutual suspicions, Saudi foreign policy elites have nonetheless treated the alternative scenario of compelling Iran to change through outright military confrontation as a non-option. It is worth noting in that spirit that the Saudi leadership has even cast its aggressive intervention in Yemen in 2015 as one they had been unwillingly forced into.[137] Some, such as Abdulrahman al-Rashid, the editor-in-chief of *Asharq al-Awsat* for 1998–2003 and manager of *Alarabiya* for 2004–2014, have even argued that the war, though waged in self-defence and at the request of the legitimate government of Yemen, was a lure by the Islamic Republic, through its proxy, to bog down and distract the Kingdom from other theatres of strategic significance.[138]

With persuasion and coercion so fraught, the near-consensus voiced among the foreign policy elites leaned towards marshalling the support of the international community to impose significant pressure on Iran. However, such coordinated containment as they understood it would not be solely aimed at limiting the Islamic Republic's nuclear or ballistic missile programmes, as had been the goal of the Obama administration and its European allies in the mid 2010s, but should include assurances and mechanisms for purposefully rolling back Iran's interference across much of the Arab world. This was the principal criticism of the JCPOA voiced by Saudi observers.[139] Al-Rashid claimed that the agreement, which was

---

[135] Awad al-Badi, 'al-'ilaqat al-su'udiyya-al-iraniyya: al-masar al-mutarib' ('Saudi–Iranian relations: an unsettled direction'), *Mokashafat* 1, no. 2 (April–June 2018): 27–28.

[136] Hossein Mousavian and Abdulaziz Sager, 'It's Time for the Leaders of Saudi Arabia and Iran to Talk', *New York Times*, 14 May 2019, www.nytimes.com/2019/05/14/opinion/saudi-arabia-iran.html.

[137] 'Liqa al-amir Mohammed bin Salman kamilan' ('The full interview with Prince Muhammad bin Salman'), AlArabiya (YouTube), 3 May 2017, www.youtube.com/watch?v=AZXSa6WZ-dA.

[138] Ranya Badawi, 'Al-katib wal mufakir al-su'udi abdulrahman al-rashid li(almasry alyoum): 'asifat al-hazm "fakh"' ('The Saudi writer and thinker Abdulrahman al-Rashid (for *Almasry alyaoum*): operation decisive storm is a "trap"'), *Almasry alyoum*, 16 May 2015, www.almasryalyoum.com/news/details/733224.

[139] 'Davos 2017 – A Conversation with Adel Al Jubeir on Middle East Security', World Economic Forum (YouTube), 21 January 2017, www.youtube.com/watch?v=FocrKQ9ZDTc; 'Keynote Address by HRH Prince Turki Al Faisal at the 2017 Arab-U.S.

'negotiated behind closed doors', was going to be the foundation for 'more dangerous wars throughout the Middle East'.[140] He noted further that those

> most angered by this agreement are the Arab states, and specifically the Gulf ones ... they were not against concluding an agreement that would end the Iranian nuclear threat, or opposed to commercial dealings with Iran, but were against the prices that were paid in exchange, most prominently giving Iran's forces a free hand to expand and battle themselves across three Arab states, Syria, Yemen, and Iraq, and to threaten the rest.[141]

This assessment is widely shared by the Saudi foreign policy elite: in one of his public talks, Prince Turki al-Faisal emphasised that a return to the JCPOA, countenanced by President Biden after the abrupt withdrawal of the US from it under the Trump administration in May 2018, should avoid the earlier mistake of neglecting the concerns of Arab states.[142] The current foreign minister, Faisal bin Farhan al-Saud, offered a similar opinion on any future internationally brokered agreement with the Islamic Republic, noting the need to avoid repeating past mistakes in engagement.[143]

All this highlights an important facet of the Saudi worldview in the 2010s – namely, the emergence of a crisis of faith in the US. Mounting differences over how to manage the Arab Spring and the Iranian threat, perceptions of an irrevocable American turn to Asia and abandonment of the region (epitomised by Obama's scathing call for Saudi Arabia to 'share the Middle East' with Iran), and a sense that there existed a sustained American media and political campaign (by 'leftist' (*yasārī*) elements) attacking the Saudi leadership following the Khashoggi incident, have all fed into this disillusionment.[144] When coupled with the attack against the

---

Policymakers Conference', National Council on U.S.-Arab Relations (YouTube), 24 October 2017, www.youtube.com/watch?v=svBktTy-404.
[140] Abdulrahman al-Rashid, 'Makhatir inhiyar itifaq iran' ('The dangers of the collapse of the agreement with Iran'), *Asharq al-Awsat*, 17 August 2017, https://short-link.me/14jAr.
[141] Al-Rashid, 'Makhatir inhiyar itifaq iran'.
[142] 'Keynote Address by Prince Turki Al Faisal (2020 Arab-US Policymakers Conference)', National Council on U.S.-Arab Relations (YouTube), 18 November 2020, www.youtube.com/watch?v=Vu39Wh-oRJo.
[143] 'Muqabala khassa ma' wazir al-kharijiyya al-su'udi faisal bin Farhan' ('A special interview with the Saudi Minister of Foreign Affairs Faisal bin Farhan'), AlArabiya (YouTube), 12 October 2022, www.youtube.com/watch?v=CjzTpXMnA0c.
[144] Abdulaziz bin Sager, 'tabayun fi wijhat al-nadar', *Asharq al-Awsat*, 5 January 2014, https://aawsat.com/home/article/16103; 'Keynote Address by HRH Prince Turki Al Faisal at the 2017 Arab-U.S. Policymakers Conference', National Council on U.S.-Arab Relations (YouTube), 24 October 2017, www.youtube.com/watch?v=svBktTy-404 'Keynote Address by Prince Turki Al Faisal (2019 Arab-US Policymakers Conference)',

oil-processing facilities at Abqaiq and Khurais in 2019, and which took place under the watch of the ostensibly friendly Trump administration, it is possible to say that Saudi foreign policy elites, traditionally pro-American in alignment, have soured on the dependability of the US as a security provider. While continuing to affirm the strategic necessity of Saudi–American relations for the country's long-term stability and security (in the words of Bin Sager, 'Riyadh is fully aware that there no realistic alternative' to the US), there is a deep apprehension that galvanises this elites' attempt (still ongoing, as of the time of writing) to procure a formalised defence treaty with the US.[145] Only an ironclad agreement could, the logic goes, affirm Saudi Arabia's status as an American allied state.

As a result of all these factors, ranging from regional disorder to American 'abandonment', Saudi foreign policy elites have gradually come to see that the responsibility for resolving these problems would be shouldered by the Kingdom, the Middle East's last major Arab power still standing. Writing as early as January 2015, Bin Sager indeed anticipated that King Salman's reign would be consumed with a task of

> filling the great strategic vacuum in the region, especially under the shadow of what are called the alternative projects. And this strategic vacuum is due to several factors: the diminishing American role in the region, and Washington relegating this role to powers unable to do it, namely Türkiye, Israel, and Iran, and the continued state of weakness that afflicts the Arab system after the so-called Arab Spring, which has been accompanied by regional polarisation and terrorist activity, and the weakness [or weakening] of the centralised state.[146]

Parsing the discourse, two simultaneous and complementary strategies are often brought up: stabilising an Arab core and engendering region-wide holistic development. The first is defined by fostering greater coordination and unity among the 'last standing' Arab states, particularly those of the GCC. In this regard, the tensions with Qatar, and their resolution

---

National Council on U.S.-Arab Relations (YouTube), 1 November 2019, www.youtube.com/watch?v=6-SPY7PCJ_s&t=679s.
Jeffrey Goldberg, 'The Obama Doctrine', *The Atlantic*, April 2016; Hesham Alghannam, 'Vision 2030: Implications for the Saudi-American Strategic Alliance', in Eleonora Ardemagni (ed.), *The Security Side of Gulf Visions: Adapting Defence to the Connectivity* (ISPI, 2024), 107–112.

[145] Abdulaziz Sager, 'The Regional and World Vision behind Saudi Transformation', in Eleonora Ardemagni (ed.), *The Security Side of Gulf Visions: Adapting Defence to the Connectivity* (ISPI, 2024), 103.

[146] Abdulaziz bin Sager, 'Al-malik salman … qiyada fi muwajahat al-tahadiyat' ('King Salman … a leadership facing many challenges'), *Asharq al-Awsat*, 28 January 2015, https://short-link.me/10d6l.

through the al-Ula reconciliation summit, have been conceptualised as bringing 'order to the [Gulf] house', a critical and powerful part of the Arab world.[147] Al-Sulami has argued that the 'Arab Gulf state system, which leads the Arab states economically, militarily, and politically must articulate an Arab project that the Arab nation can gather around in order to ... confront these three projects [the Iranian, Turkish, and Israeli], which aim to swallow the Arab region, albeit at different levels and degrees.'[148] Within this framework, the Saudi state, at the self-perceived head of the Gulf collective, would endeavour to build a security coalition capable of resisting the encroachments of others – be they Iranian or otherwise – and offering a new vision for the wider Arab world.

This brings us to the second strategy, that of development, which itself is entangled with Vision 2030. As indicated by the Crown Prince from his very first public appearance, the national transformation of the Kingdom overrides all other issues and priorities.[149] Faisal bin Farhan – prior to his appointment at the top of the Ministry of Foreign Affairs but during his assumption of an advisory role at the royal court – also argued that internal development was now the focus of the Saudi leadership, and that this would have foreign policy repercussions, reinforcing, for instance, the pursuit of non-confrontational options.[150] By enhancing the resilience and sustainability of the Saudi state and political economy, as well as harnessing some degree of self-sufficiency in military and technological production, the purpose of Vision 2030, as Alghannam puts it, is purposefully that of 'strengthening the internal front in a region thronged by failed states'.[151]

Saudi foreign policy elites see internal development as breaking the deadlock across the wider Middle East, and in creating a pathway for

---

[147] Abdulaziz bin Sager, 'al-tawafuq al-khaliji ... bayn al-waqi' wal mamul' ('Gulf comity ... between reality and hope'), *Asharq al-Awsat*, 13 March 2014, https://aawsat.com/home/article/55006; 'Keynote Address by HRH Prince Turki Al Faisal at the 2016 Arab-U.S. Policymakers Conference', National Council on U.S.-Arab Relations (YouTube), 8 November 2016, www.youtube.com/watch?v=rNoh5fO4Q7o&t=921s; 'Nas bunud al-bayan al-khitami al-117 al-sadir 'an al-qima al-khalijiyya fi al-'ula' ('Text for the clauses of the finalized 117th Statement from the Gulf Summit in Al-'Ula'), *Asharq al-Awsat*, 5 January 2021, https://short-link.me/14jAQ.

[148] Muhammad bin Sagr al-Sulami, 'Mustaqbal al-'ilaqat al-su'udiyya al-iraniyya': 108.

[149] 'Mohammed bin Salman fi awal muqabalah 'ala al-'arabiyya' ('Mohammed bin Salman in his first interview with al-'Arabiyya') AlArabiya (YouTube), 25 April 2016, www.youtube.com/watch?v=uhWfUK0aizw.

[150] 'Saudi Arabia Transforming: Keynote with Prince Faisal Bin Farhan Al-Saud', Arab Gulf States Institute in Washington (YouTube), 10 May 2017, www.youtube.com/watch?v=Q0jM8EFmfKs&t=348s.

[151] Hisham Alghannam, 'Al-tahawut al-su'udi ... al-qabil li at-tafawudh wa 'aksih' ('Saudi hedging ... what is negotiable and what is not'), *Asharq al-Awsat*, 27 December 2020, https://short-link.me/14jAZ.

stabilisation. Alghannam noted in the same commentary that 'there is a deep and pragmatic Saudi conviction of the connection between prosperity and the reinforcement of security, as a region that is more stable and prosperous will be more capable of reigning in, and diminishing, the threat posed by Iran'.[152] Some elites have gone even further, contrasting the renaissance being experienced in the Kingdom with the Islamic Republic's descent into stagnation and turmoil in recent years, an asymmetry that they believe has diminished Iranian capacity to compete with Saudi soft power.[153] Some even suggest, as did Faisal bin Farhan, that Iran could be offered an opportunity to partake in the fruits of Saudi Arabia's economic rise if its leadership renounces its hostile foreign policy.[154] ʿAziz Alghashiʿan, a Saudi analyst, has opined along similar lines, arguing that Vision 2030 is a de-escalatory instrument of Saudi foreign policy that has the potential to create new incentives for problematic regional players such as Iran and Israel.[155]

The twin strategies are defensive responses to an unstable regional environment and are suggestive of the limitations – in power projection, resilience, and in the range of security and diplomatic options available – that Saudi Arabia confronts. At their heart is the aspirational idea that by shoring up and amplifying what remains of Arab power, as embodied by the Kingdom and, to a lesser extent, the rest of the GCC, and relying on development, the catalysts of turbulence in the Middle East could be tackled and, consequently, a new regional order based on respect for the sovereignty and integrity of all its constituent nation-state actors might be brought into being.

China in the Saudi Worldview

Saudi foreign policy elites traditionally espoused a broad range of views regarding the PRC, including those of a critical and negative nature, in the early decades immediately following the establishment of diplomatic relations in 1990.[156] Some of these represented continuities with past criticisms of the PRC harkening back to the narratives of the Cold War, but others also

---

[152] Alghannam, 'Al-tahawut al-suʾudi ... al-qabil li at-tafawudh wa ʿaksih'.
[153] Conversations at the Prince Saud al-Faisal Institute in Riyadh, Saudi Arabia (14 June 2023).
[154] 'Muqabala khassa maʿ wazir al-kharijiyya al-suʾudi faisal bin Farhan', AlArabiya (YouTube), 12 October 2022, www.youtube.com/watch?v=CjzTpXMnA0c.
[155] Aziz Alghasian, 'The Saudi Tool for Middle East Stability: Vision 2030 Reshapes Relations with Iran and Israel', in Eleonora Ardemagni (ed.), *The Security Side of Gulf Visions: Adapting Defence to the Connectivity* (ISPI, 2024), 115–121.
[156] Mohammed Turki Al-Sudairi, 'China in the Eyes of the Saudi Media', GRC Gulf Papers, February 2013.

reflected a tone of dissatisfaction with (what was then) unfamiliar Chinese foreign policy.¹⁵⁷ Influential commentators such as al-Rashid – a royal court whisperer well known for his pro-American stance – either dismissed or attacked Beijing's actions (or inaction) with regards to different regional issues, such as the Darfur crisis in Sudan and regime change in Syria.¹⁵⁸

By the mid 2010s, the spectrum of opinions on the PRC shifted towards a more positive direction as Sino-Saudi ties strengthened and new domestic and regional imperatives came to the fore. Saudi foreign policy elites have increasingly toned down their negative treatments of Chinese foreign policy, with criticisms on sensitive topics (such as Chinese policies in XUAR) mostly disappearing in turn. Recent scholarship on media and popular coverage of the PRC in Saudi Arabia confirms this overall development.¹⁵⁹ Instead, the elites have come to stress the fundamental overlaps in perspectives – such as an abiding respect for Westphalian sovereignty and a focus on economic development – that exist between the two sides. In an address given at Peking University in 2016, al-Jubeir declared such alignments in value as part of a 'common philosophy' shared by the Kingdom and the PRC.¹⁶⁰

Within the Saudi foreign policy elite discourse, the PRC is imagined to exercise a positive influence, though principally through its economic heft.¹⁶¹ Domestically, economic relations have consistently been viewed as a vital element in sustaining Vision 2030, an unsurprising claim if one considers the value of Chinese energy imports from Saudi Arabia and, with the PRC being the largest market for Saudi oil since 2011, how much policymakers in Riyadh depend on the revenues accrued from them (Figure 8).¹⁶² Regionally, the PRC is, to borrow from al-Jubeir, envisioned

---

¹⁵⁷ Alsudairi, 'Forging an Anti-Bandung'.
¹⁵⁸ Abdulrahman al-Rashid, 'Al-mukhadir al-sini wal naft al-sudani' ('The Chinese opiate and the Sudanese oil'), *Asharq al-Awsat*, 24 February 2008, https://short-link.me/14jBa; Abdulrahman al-Rashid, 'Mahazil: tabaru' al-sin wa quwat al-'arabi' ('Ridiculousness: China's donation and the power of the Arab'), *Asharq al-Awsat*, 14 January 2013, https://short-link.me/10d6U.
¹⁵⁹ Shahram Akbarzadeh and Arif Saba, 'China's Soft Power: Views from Saudi Arabia and the UAE', *Global Studies Quarterly* 5, no. 1 (January 2025): 1–14; Andrew Leber, 'Seek Fact from Texts: Saudi Media on China amid the COVID-19 Pandemic', *Asian Journal of Middle Eastern and Islamic Studies* 14, no. 4 (2020): 538–553.
¹⁶⁰ 'Muhadarat ma' ali al-wazir fi jami'at bikeen bi'inwan: al-'ilaqat al-su'udiyya- al-siniyya 31 August 2016' ('Lecture of His Excellency in Peking University under the title: Saudi–Chinese Relations'), Ministry of Foreign Affairs of Saudi Arabia (YouTube), 3 September 2016, www.youtube.com/watch?v=wP0oZTEv57Q&t=631s.
¹⁶¹ Many of the talking points about the PRC's economic prowess are often regurgitations of what one finds in older media debates from the 2000s; see Mohammed Turki Al-Sudairi, 'China in the Eyes of the Saudi Media', GRC Gulf Papers, February 2013.
¹⁶² Christopher S. Chivvis, Aaron David Miller, and Beatrix Geaghan-Breiner, 'Saudi Arabia in the Emerging World Order', Carnegie Endowment, 6 November 2023,

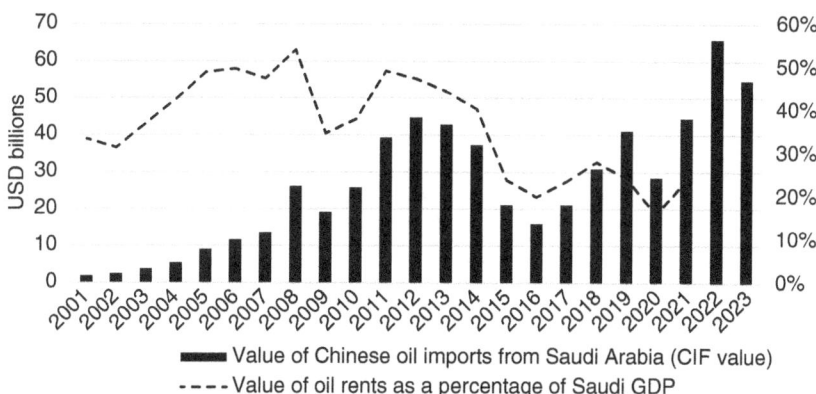

Figure 8 Sino-Saudi energy relations and the Saudi economy.
Source: Compiled by the authors using data from the World Bank and from the International Trade Centre.

as a 'force of stability' – an actor that trades with everyone and adheres to a predictable state- and business-centric approach in dealing not only with the Kingdom but the Middle East more broadly.[163] The Riyadh Declaration issued at the conclusion of the first Sino-Arab summit in December 2022 called for greater Chinese and regional coordination in addressing lingering conflicts while also stressing the need for continued economic cooperation.[164] Capturing the essence of the Saudi and Chinese approaches to the dilemmas of the Middle East, it stated that 'there is no peace without sustainable development, and no development and prosperity without security' – the latter being achieved through mediational resolutions that are tied to greater economic integrationist projects, whether that of the BRI or Vision 2030.

A demonstrative example of the PRC's stabilising role through the power of economics is the widespread narrative among the Saudi elites that their acceptance of a détente with Iran was predicated upon the view that Beijing, by virtue of its extensive political and economic ties with Tehran, could

---

https://carnegieendowment.org/research/2023/11/saudi-arabia-in-the-emerging-world-order?lang=en; 'Saudi Arabia', ChinaMed, undated, www.chinamed.it/chinamed-data/middle-east/saudi-arabia.

[163] 'Davos 2017 – A Conversation with Adel Al Jubeir on Middle East Security', World Economic Forum (YouTube), 21 January 2017, www.youtube.com/watch?v=FocrKQ9ZDTc.

[164] 'Sudur "ilan al-riyadh" an qimat al-riyadh al-'arabiyya al-siniyya lil ta'awun wal tanmiyya' ('Issuance of the "Riyadh Declaration" about the Riyadh Arab–Chinese Summit for Cooperation and Development'), (Saudi) Ministry of Foreign Affairs, 9 December 2022, https://short-link.me/14jBA.

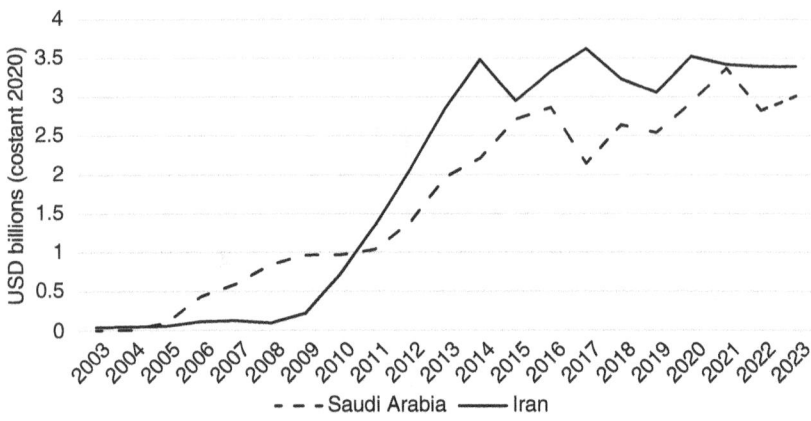

Figure 9 Chinese foreign direct investment (stock) in Iran and Saudi Arabia.

Source: Compiled by the authors using data from the Chinese Ministry of Commerce, China National Bureau of Statistics, and the State Administration of Foreign Exchange.

not only pressure them to comply but also had a real stake in guaranteeing its realisation that any violation of the agreement would put its economic interests in the Gulf on the line.[165] Figure 9 clearly shows the foundation of this thinking, with the Kingdom, for example, recently catching up with the Islamic Republic in attracting Chinese capital after lagging behind for many years. Whether the PRC, as an untested diplomatic power, is actually able to deliver on the guarantees of the détente is an open question for some commentators like al-Rashid, but the Chinese-brokered agreement is worth a serious attempt, he would argue, as '[the Saudis] are realists, but at the same time, optimists'.[166] If it holds, it would partially address one of the principal causes of instability in the Middle East (Iranian expansionism) or at least its specific threat to the Kingdom, while also allowing the

---

[165] There has always been some degree of discomfort with Sino-Iranian relations, especially following news of the twenty-five-year strategic agreement. However, many Saudi observers have come to view the PRC's strong ties with Saudi Arabia, its inherent ideological tensions with Iran (on foreign policy), and the imperative of ensuring unimpeded energy imports from the region as placing real restrictions on the extent of Chinese support to Iran. For a comprehensive analysis of Saudi discourse on Sino-Iranian relations, see Houghton, 'China's Balancing Strategy between Saudi Arabia and Iran'; Abdulrahman al-Rashid, 'Al-sin wa amrika fi al-khalij', *Asharq al-Awsat*, 2 April 2021, https://short-link.me/14jBH; Abdulrahman al-Rashid, '"Bikeen" hal yunhi niza' 40 'aman?' ('Will Beijing end a fight of forty years?'), *Asharq al-Awsat*, 11 March 2023. https://short-link.me/14jBW.

[166] Abdulrahman al-Rashid, '"Bikeen" hal yunhi niza' 40 aman? (2)' ('Will Beijing end a fight of forty years?'), *Asharq al-Awsat*, 15 March 2023.

PRC to continue facilitating region-wide economic integration through the BRI – all of which are outcomes that dovetail with Saudi Arabia's strategies to refashion the regional order.[167]

Notwithstanding the great emphasis placed in the discourse on the PRC as an economic power, what is absent is any serious discussion of it playing a security role, with military power as a key component, akin to that of the role that the US plays. At best, as the ever-sceptical al-Rashid notes, the PRC's embrace of a more active security role could come about in the far future, with the Chinese, in response to their ever-growing interests, following in the footsteps of their Portuguese, British, and American imperial predecessors.[168] However, it is clear that Saudi commentators are cognisant that the PRC has little appetite for such responsibilities, with some, like al-Dowsari, opining that any large-scale Chinese involvement in the region's security affairs would only come about as part of a Saudi-led multilateral initiative, and would thus be distinct from traditional US patterns of security engagement in the Middle East.[169] They do not see this as a tenable scenario now or in the future, and appear to be aware of the limits of what the PRC could realistically do in the region.

That said, outright alignment with the PRC, entailing an alliance or adoption of the Chinese yuan, is sometimes brought up in the discourse

---

[167] 'Keynote Address by Prince Turki Al Faisal at the 27th Annual Arab-U.S. Policymakers Conference 2018', KFCRIS (YouTube), 1 November 2018, www.youtube.com/watch?v=5PRo3yS1Cr0; 'Saudi Arabia's Foreign Policy Directions, by Prince Faisal bin Farhan Al Saud', Institut français des relations internationals (YouTube), 14 December 2022, www.youtube.com/watch?v=zrggxoUF-vE; 'Muqabala khassa ma' wazir al-kharijiyya al-su'udi faisal bin Farhan', AlArabiya (YouTube), 12 October 2022, www.youtube.com/watch?v=CjzTpXMnA0c; Salman al-Dowsari, 'bayn al-su'udiyya wal sin … ruya wa hizam wa tariq' ('Between Saudi Arabia and China … is a vision, determination, and a path'), *Asharq al-Awsat*, 10 December 2022, https://short-link.me/14jCl.

[168] Abdulrahman al-Rashid, 'Hal hiya nihayat al-khilaf al-su'udi al-amriki?' ('Is this the end of the Saudi–American disagreement?'), *Asharq al-Awsat*, 10 March 2023, https://short-link.me/14jCs.

[169] Abdulrahman al-Rashid, 'Al-sin mustaqbalna' ('China is our future'), *Asharq al-Awsat*, 4 September 2016, https://short-link.me/14jCx. In this editorial, al-Rashid was responding to public rumors that Kuwait had agreed to host Chinese naval bases on its islands in exchange for economic benefits and security guarantees. Abdulrahman al-Rashid, 'Al-siniyun min iran ila al-khalij' ('The Chinese from Iraq to the Gulf'), *Asharq al-Awsat*, 16 July 2018, https://short-link.me/14jCJ; Mohammed Al-Sudairi, 'The Curious Case of China's 'Kuwaiti Concession', The Arab Gulf States Institute in Washington, 10 October 2018, https://agsiw.org/the-curious-case-of-chinas-kuwaiti-concession/; Salman al-Dowsari, 'Al-malik salman fi asiya … tariq al-harir al-jadid' ('King Salman in Asia … the new Silk Road'), *Asharq al-Awsat*, 2 March 2017, https://short-link.me/14jD1; Salman al-Dowsari, 'Al-sharaka al-su'udiyya ma' al-numur al-asyawiyya' ('The Saudi partnership with the Asian Tigers'), *Asharq al-Awsat*, 26 June 2019, https://short-link.me/14jDb.

of Saudi foreign policy elites, though rather opaquely and almost always exclusively in discussions surrounding Saudi–American relations. The statements of the Crown Prince, in his 2018 and 2022 interviews with *The Atlantic*, or that of Turki al-Dakhil (the current Saudi ambassador to the United Arab Emirates), in an infamous and bombastic editorial threatening a radical turn towards Russia and the PRC, are illustrative in that regard.[170] Such commentary can only be read against the backdrop of the deterioration in American-Saudi (and Sino-American) relations: Saudi foreign policy elites are consciously leveraging concerns in Washington about great power competition with the PRC in the Middle East for their own purposes,[171] a strategy that is certainly not new in previous periods of strain.[172] By raising the spectre of a possible Saudi dash to Beijing, they aim not only to arrest the tensions in Saudi–American ties but also to breathe new strategic life into their security partnership: the Kingdom, after all, is seeking a defence treaty with the US, not the PRC. This confirms the primacy of the US in the thinking of Saudi foreign policy elites, an appraisal that will likely endure even if the current round of treaty-negotiations fails to bear fruit. What emerges then is a bifurcated allotment of roles as far as the great powers are concerned, with the US for security and the PRC for the economy.

On the Saudi Vision

In this section, we have examined how Saudi foreign policy elites understand the situation in the Middle East, as well as their evaluations of the PRC's role there. Across the board, they see a collapsed regional order brought about by the subversive activities of ideologically driven

---

[170] Jeffrey Goldberg, 'Saudi Crown Prince: Iran's Supreme Leader "Makes Hitler Look Good"', *The Atlantic*, 2 April 2018, www.theatlantic.com/international/archive/2018/04/mohammed-bin-salman-iran-israel/557036/; Turki al-Dakhil, 'Al-'uqubat al-amrikiyya 'ala al-riyadh ta'ni an washintun tat'an nafsaha' ('American sanctions on Riyadh mean that Washington is stabbing itself'), *Asharq al-Awsat*, 14 October 2018, https://short-link.me/14jDj; Graeme Woods, 'Absolute Power', *The Atlantic*, 3 March 2022, https://short-link.me/10d98.

[171] As Jon Alterman has astutely observed when discussing recent Saudi–American reproachment, 'How do you keep China from aligning with Saudi Arabia? You have a relationship ... Part of the argument ... is you couldn't abandon the Middle East to China, and the Saudis reminded the administration of the Chinese option at every opportunity they got.' In Felicia Schwartz and Andrew England, 'How the Saudis Won Back Biden', *The Financial Times*, 17 June 2024.

[172] Prince Turki al-Faisal's comment from 2006, '[I]s China a better friend to Saudi Arabia than the United States is? Not necessarily a better friend, but a less complicated friend', comes to mind, see *USA Today*, 2006, A13.

(state and non-state) actors, on the one hand, and the governance and developmental failures of Arab elites, on the other. As the last remaining Arab power of consequence, and with a perception of US withdrawal, many of them had come to the conclusion in the 2010s that Saudi Arabia should adopt a robust strategy of reformational self-strengthening coupled with an activist foreign policy that places a premium on fostering cooperation and economic integration across the Middle East. The story they have come to embrace is one in which the Kingdom is increasingly at the centre of reconstituting the Middle East after a drawn-out period of chaos and instability, reasserting in some ways a natural position of leadership in this environment.

Within this remedial vision, the PRC is valued for its stabilising role, particularly in the economic domain, an appraisal that interestingly displays parallels with that of Chinese foreign policy elites and confirms the claim (irrespective of its propagandistic import) of a common philosophy existing between the two sides. At the same time, there is clearly no expectation that the PRC will take on a security role. The US remains, to all intents and purposes, and as a matter of consensus, the only real alternative, despite all the tensions that mar Saudi–American relations. The significance of all this is that Saudi foreign policy elites, though adhering to the vision that the region is undergoing great change that has necessitated the wholesale reformation of the Kingdom itself, do not anticipate any major departures in Chinese foreign policy in the Middle East over the short or mid-term and are seemingly satisfied and content with it so far. It should be noted that the PRC's tangible economic importance for Saudi foreign policy elites is supplemented by its political function as a 'scarecrow' in the context of the Kingdom's relationship with the US, inadvertently breathing new life into the latter while also providing space for further strategic manoeuvrings by Riyadh as it charts a new course for itself within the regional order. In that sense, Saudi foreign policy elites are seeking to forestall a post-American Middle East, but are preparing for such a scenario nevertheless.

Assadist Syria: Waiting for a New Regional Order

This section examines how the changes in the Middle East regional order, and the PRC's place within it as an extra-regional great power, have been perceived in Assadist Syria. It is apparent that for much of the past decade, the thinking of Assadist Syrian foreign policy elites was haunted by the existential fear of regime collapse. Beleaguered and facing a devastating nexus of external and internal threats, they depicted the drawn-out crisis of the civil war as a 'global conspiracy' (*al-muāmara al-kawniyya*) orchestrated by the US and its allies to extinguish Baʿthist rule over Syria and spread imperialist control over the remaining strongholds of the anti-American 'resistance' (*al-muqāwama*) in the Middle East.

Weathering this sustained assault was therefore given the utmost priority by Assadist Syrian foreign policy elites, who viewed the 2010s as a critical turning point in which their country was on the precipice of collapse, and the regional order was in a liminal state of flux between achieving real 'sovereign decision-making' (*istiqlāl al-qarār*) and falling into the American empire's orbit under conditions of 'vassalage' (*tabaʿiyya*). Within this context, the PRC – cast in the role of an ascendant antagonist to the US – was imagined as providing, along with Russia and Iran, a capacity to resist the latter outcome through diplomatic, financial, and even military means.

This was by no means an asymmetric dynamic: by aiding Syria in its 'battle of resilience' (*maʿrakat al-sumūd*) against American-led regime-change and emboldening regional rejectionism, Assadist Syrian foreign policy elites came to argue that this advanced the PRC's interests in so far as the US was no longer able to commit all of its resources towards containment and strategic re-positioning in East Asia. Within the scope of this narration, Sino-Syrian relations were envisioned as contributing to the emergence of a new post-American regional, even global, order, albeit without invoking any specific claims of how Chinese involvement in the regional security architecture would express itself.

Syria as Victim, the Region as Battleground

Assadist Syrian foreign policy elites have voiced a relatively consistent worldview throughout the 2010s. A unifying feature of their discourse is the envisioning of Syria, drawing on classical Baʿthist language, as the 'beating heart of Arabism' (*qalb al-ʿuruba al-nābidh*). The values of independence and sovereignty (for the Syrian and Arab peoples) meant that Syria could only but embrace a foreign policy defined by 'rejectionism' (*mumānaʿa*) of American hegemony in the Middle East and 'confrontation' (*muwājaha*) with Israeli occupation (in the Golan Heights, Palestine proper, and elsewhere).[173] For these elites, Syria had not capitulated to the spirit of 'defeatism' (*inhizāmiyya*) that had afflicted its Arab surroundings.

---

[173] Bente Scheller, *The Wisdom of Syria's Waiting Game: Foreign Policy under the Assads* (Hurst, 2013).

Because of its honourable and unwavering 'stances' (*mawāqif*) on behalf of the Syrian (and Arab) peoples, and its refusal to accept US diktats, the country was subject to immense punishment that rendered it, in the conception of Assadist Syrian foreign policy elites, a martyr and victim.[174]

This does not mean that the Assadist leadership viewed itself as being driven by anti-American obscurantism, but rather that it was willing to reach an accommodation with the US without sacrificing its core national interests (and those of the wider Arab nation). We can discern this from how Syrian–American negotiations in the 1980s–1990s were depicted and commemorated: Buthayna Sha'ban,[175] the longstanding political and media adviser to the presidency and principal mouthpiece of the regime, who has now fled the country with the fall of Bashar al-Assad, published three Arabic and English books that emphasised Hafiz al-Assad's identity as a peacemaker who had been ultimately frustrated by American disregard for the legitimate and sovereign rights of Syria and Palestine.[176]

Because of these stances, regime change in Syria – and the consequent abdication of core Arab causes – is linked to the triumph of foreign (namely, American) interests. As recently as 2023, Bashar al-Assad repeated a common talking point that while yielding to the US might have brought peace to the land, it would have extracted 'a greater price we [in Syria] would have had to pay later on' due to the inherent injustice of its demands.[177] This high cost has meant that calls for regime change, especially in the form of democratisation, could never have emanated from genuinely

---

[174] 'Al-assad yatrah halan siyasiyyan lil azma min thalathat marahil wa yuakid: suriyya satabqa kama kanat wa sata'ud' ('Al-Assad puts forward a political solution to the crisis comprised of three phases, and confirms: Syria will remain as it was, and will return'), SANA, 7 January 2013, www.sana.sy/?p=3139; 'Al-'iraq ... al-maydan al-badil lil 'udwan ... wal radd?' SANA, 23 June 2014, www.sana.sy/?p=7646; 'Hiwar khass – buthayna Sha'ban – al-mustashara al-i'lamiyya wa al-siyasiyya liriasa al-suriyya – 03-03-2014' ('Special conversation – Buthayna Sha'ban – the media and political consultant to the Syrian Presidency'), Al-Mayadeen (YouTube), 4 March 2014, www.youtube.com/watch?v=sRXfyfAyfIM.

[175] For a fascinating sketch of her intellectual journey, see Asaad Al-Saleh, 'Failing the Masses: Buthaina Shabaan and the Public Intellectual Crisis', *Journal of International Women's Studies* 13, no. 5 (2012): 195–211.

[176] 'Ma ba'da al-'ard / halaqa khassa ma' buthana sha'ban / 02-11-2018' ('After the presentation/special interview with Buthayna Sha'ban/02-11-2018'), Al-Mayadeen (YouTube), 3 November 2018, www.youtube.com/watch?v=OyHQ1gKE-2E; 'Al-doktora sha'ban: suriyya bisumudiha wa intisariha qadamat anamuthajan lil 'alam bina iradat al-shu'ub la tuqhar' ('Dr Sha'ban: through its perseverance and triumph Syria has given the world a model in which the will of the people cannot be vanquished'), SANA, 10 May, www.sana.sanasyria.org/?p=1379006.

[177] 'Muqabala hasriyya ma' al-rais al-suri bashar al-assad 'ala skynews 'arabiyya' ('A special interview with the Syrian President Bashar al-Assad on Sky News Arabia'), Sky News 'Arabiyya (YouTube), 10 August 2023, www.youtube.com/watch?v=cQrVbS0Cg2c.

patriotic Syrian elements, but rather fifth-columnists that sought to serve Washington and its allies.[178] Accordingly, the civil war that raged for much of the 2010s could only be interpreted as foreign perfidy and conspiratorial machination: during al-Assad's infamous address at the National Assembly in 2011 – his first public appearance after the outbreak of popular demonstrations against his rule – he attributed the unrest to the instigation of outsiders who wanted 'strife' (*fitna*) and the end of Ba'ath Party rule.[179]

Though the US is identified by Syrian foreign policy elites as the main culprit, the attack on Syria had taken on 'universal' (*kawniyya*) proportions, involving Israel, other regional 'comprador-allies' (Türkiye, Egypt, and the Gulf monarchies) of the West, as well as an assortment of extremist Islamist groups such as al-Qaeda and ISIL.[180] Spearheaded by 'a vile and terroristic excommunicatory aggression backed by the fake democracies and medieval sheikdoms', this coalition, to borrow from the assistant to the foreign minister, Ayman Sawsan, has sought to destroy Syria and breach the last standing stronghold of Arabism.[181] Using similar language, Faysal al-Miqdad, a long-serving Syrian diplomat and one-time foreign minister, has claimed that a core Israeli–Saudi alliance, with US backing, has endeavoured to punish Syria and compel it to join a regional order that has largely accepted US diktats.[182]

---

[178] 'Al-rais al-assad li qanat khabar al-iraniyya: tasrihat al-masulin al-gharbiyyin al-ijabiyya wal salibiyya la yumkin akhthha 'ala mahmal al-jid li 'adam al-thiqa bihim … al-juhud al-suriyya al-rusiyya al-iraniyya al-'iraqiyya yajib an yuktab laha al-najah fi mukafahat al-irhab wa illa fanahnu amam tadmir mantiqa bi akmaliha' ('President al-Assad to the Iranian al-Khabar News Channel: the positive and negative comments of Western officials cannot be taken seriously as they are not trustworthy … the Syrian, Russian, Iranian, and Iraqi efforts must succeed in combating terrorism or otherwise we face the destruction of the whole region'), SANA, 4 October 2015, www.sana.sy/?p=278324.

[179] 'Khitab al-rais al-suri bashar al-assad fi majlis al-sha'b' ('The address of Syrian President Bashar al-Assad in the People's Assembly'), Al-Jadeed News (YouTube), 31 March 2011, www.youtube.com/watch?v=S89q-tVZp0o.

[180] 'Al-miqdad: ma tata'arad lahu suriya huwa 'idwan yahmil fi kul tafasilihi sifat al-'udwan al-khariji' ('Al-Miqdad: What Syria faces is aggression that carries the characteristic of a foreign aggression'), SANA, 28 June 2014, www.sana.sy/?p=11012; 'Muqabalat al-rais al-assad ma' finiks al-siniyya' ('Interview of President al-Assad with Chinese Phoenix TV'), Syrian Presidency (YouTube), 16 September 2018, www.youtube.com/watch?v=rqH60rwEEaY; 'Muqabala hasriyya ma' al-rais al-suri bashar al-assad 'ala skynews 'arabiyya' ('A special interview with Syrian President Bashar al-Assad on Sky News Arabia') SkyNews 'Arabiyya (YouTube), 10 August 2023, www.youtube.com/watch?v=cQrVbS0Cg2c.

[181] 'Safir al-sin bidimashq: mubadarat al-rais al-assad lil tawajuh sharqan tatawafaq ma' al-mubara al-siniyya (al-tariq wal hizam)' ('The Chinese Ambassador in Damascus: the initiative of President al-Assad to orient eastward accords with the Chinese Initiative (Belt and Road)'), SANA, 25 September 2017, www.sana.sy/?p=631821.

[182] 'Hadith Dimashq – faysal miqdad – naib wazir al-kharijiyya al-suri – 30-11-2013' ('Damascus Conversations – Faysal Miqdad – Syrian Vice Minister of the Ministry of

As can be gleaned from the discourse espoused by Assadist Syrian foreign policy elites, the main predicament facing the regional order was the US bid to establish uncontested hegemony over it. According to this worldview, the Americans embraced a strategy of 'creative chaos' (*fawdha khalāqa*) since the late 1990s and early 2000s, entailing the use of terrorism, so-called democracy promotion, and even outright war (as was the case with Baʿathist Iraq), all of which were purposed towards pre-empting any improvements in Arab or regional affairs.[183] As would be expected, this strategy was not used solely against Syria but targeted many other revisionist forces in the Middle East, including Iran, post-Saddam Iraq, Hizbollah in Lebanon, the Houthīs in Yemen, and various Palestinian factions, such as Hamas. In the words of Hizbollah cadre-officials (reproduced in SANA), the American threat brought all of these actors together in the shared cause of 'resistance' (*muqāwamah*) to the imposition of an 'American-Israeli project' (*al-mashruʾ al-amrīkī al-israilī*) in the Middle East – namely, that of eviscerating any challengers to American hegemony and the Zionist settler-colonial enterprise in Palestine.[184] As al-Assad puts it, the project is about ensuring the formation of fragmented, weak, and compliant states that cannot be concerned with whatever happens beyond their borders.[185] For al-Miqdad, what the US wants for the region is simply 'evil' (*al-sharr*).[186]

Though the enemy is conceived as all-powerful and cruel, the Manichean discourse of the Assadist Syrian foreign policy elites treated Syria and its allies, due to their righteousness and tenacity, as an inevitably victorious cohort. With quasi-spiritual certainty, they viewed their country's continued survival as a rebuke to American unipolarity, placing limits on its imperial reach and ensuring that parts of the Middle East remained free

---

Foreign Affairs'), Al Mayadeen Programs (YouTube), 1 December 2013, www.youtube.com/watch?v=LiOvyYBHbh0.

[183] 'Vidyu muqabalat al-rais al-asad maʾ finiks al-siniyya' ('Video of President al-Assad's Interview with Chinese Phoenix TV'), Syrian Presidency (YouTube), 16 December 2019, www.youtube.com/watch?v=QkN7HWIsfF8.

[184] 'Qasim: al-mashruʾ al-irhabi al-takfiri yastahdif al-jamiʾ wal muqawamah hiya al-hal al-awal limuwajahatih' ('Qasim: The excommunicatory and terrorist project targets everyone and the resistance is the solution to contend with it'), SANA, 30 December 2014, www.sana.sy/?p=123511; 'Amin al-Sayyid: al-mashruʾ al-amriki al-sahyuni sayasqut fi suriyya' ('Amin al-Sayyid: the American-Zionist project will fall in Syria'), SANA, 10 August 2017, www.sana.sy/?p=604350.

[185] 'Al-rais al-assad li qanat khabar al-iraniyya.'

[186] 'Liqa d. Faysal miqdad wazir al-kharijiyya wal mughtaribin dhimn barnamaj nuwuyzmaykar' ('Meeting with Dr Faysal al-Miqdad, Vice Minister of the Ministry of Foreign Affairs and Expatriates in the NewsMaker Programme'), BTV (YouTube), 23 May 2024, www.youtube.com/watch?v=y7-g7wzAm34&t=474s.

of its control.¹⁸⁷ Indeed, it is Syria and its allies who protected the rest of the region from total destruction (especially from US-backed terrorism, typified by Dāʿish expansionism in the mid 2010s).¹⁸⁸ In the *longue durée* of history, this is nothing new. In an interview with CCTV, al-Assad stated that Syria had been on the path of many foreign invasions in the past (alluding to the Crusaders and Mongols) but that it always prevailed in the end.¹⁸⁹ Elsewhere both he and Sha'ban asserted that Syria had effectively triumphed in the 'long war' being waged against it: the US project of vassalising the country had floundered.¹⁹⁰

This inherent optimism about Syria's present and future ability to resist the pressures of being incorporated into an American imperium was replicated with respect to the regional order, and particularly those segments of it that had traditionally been seen to lie within the US sphere of influence. In the Arab League summit held in May 2023, al-Assad gave a short address, the first in such a forum in more than a decade since Syria's expulsion, that struck such a note.¹⁹¹ He argued that while Arab states still faced many threats, including neo-Ottoman expansionism and chronic underdevelopment, recent Arab- and regional-level reconciliations, as well as renewed commitments to non-interference and sovereignty, meant that the Arab collective could begin to seriously (and advantageously) capitalise on an increasingly multipolar (*mutʿadid al-aqṭāb*) global landscape. An Arab recovery no longer subject to the will of the US was now a realistic possibility. Saudi Arabia, criticised in the 2010s as one of the most benighted and destructive of those 'following the US agenda', was now praised for its independent foreign policy and re-engagement with the axis of resistance (typified by the Saudi–Iranian détente), a development indicative of the decline of American power throughout the region.¹⁹²

---

[187] 'Al-doktora sha'ban: suriyya bisumudiha wa intisariha qadamat anamuthajan lil 'alam bina iradat al-shu'ub la tuqhar'.

[188] 'Al-rais al-assad li qanat khabar al-iraniyya'.

[189] 'Muqabalat al-sayyid al-rais bashar al-assad ma' tilvizyun al-sin al-markazi' ('The interview of His Excellency the President Bashar al-Assad with China's Central TV'), Syrian Presidency (YouTube), 30 September 2023, www.youtube.com/watch?v=mqkqj_SF-zs.

[190] 'Muqabala hasriyya ma' al-rais al-suri bashar al-assad 'ala skynews 'arabiyya' ('A special interview with the Syrian President Bashar al-Assad on Sky News Arabia'), Sky News 'Arabiyya (YouTube), 10 August 2023, www.youtube.com/watch?v=cQrVbS0Cg2c.

[191] 'Bashar al-assad: ashkur al-su'udiyya lita'ziz al-musalaha fi mantiqatina' ('Bashar al-Assad: I thank Saudi Arabia for reinforcing reconciliation in our region'), Al-Jadeed News (YouTube), 23 May 2023, www.youtube.com/watch?v=VHI8hMKuVW0.

[192] 'Al-rais al-assad li sahifat tishrin: aham shay fi harb tishrin huwa intisar al-irada wal 'aql al-arabi 'ala al-khawf wal awham ... akbar intisar al-yaum huwa an naqdhi 'ala al-irhabiyin wal fikr al-irhabi' ('President al-Assad to Tishrin Newspaper: the most important thing in the Tishrin war was the victory of the Arab will and mind over fear and delusions ...

As is clear, the notion of multipolarity – with Russia and the PRC (and to a lesser extent, Iran) at the helm – is central to Assadist Syrian foreign policy discourse in so far as it is understood to be the principal factor that had enabled Syria's survival, on the one hand, and the catalyst behind the transformations taking place within the regional order, on the other.[193] Much like the way in which the US in the Middle East brought disparate actors together in resistance, the world-spanning scope of the American imperial project, extending from Latin America to East Asia, tied the axis of the region with likeminded (and increasingly powerful) actors from other faraway places who themselves were free of 'Western colonial thinking' (al-tafkīr al-isti'mārī al-gharbī).[194] As al-Assad readily noted in his interview with the Tishrīn newspaper, non-Western alternatives and blocs were not seriously considered until the full weight of the American challenge was felt by Syria as it descended into civil war.[195]

Assadist Syrian foreign policy elites have accordingly moved to interpret and justify the interventions of external actors on their country's behalf as signs of a shared anti-imperialist struggle that belies the wider systemic changes brought into motion by great powers such as Russia and the PRC. They viewed this as is an unstoppable trend and one that strengthened, and drew strength from, Syria's own victory on the domestic battlefront. In an interview with Russia Today (reproduced in SANA), al-Assad commented that 'we have always believed that whenever Russia is stronger – and I do not just speak with Syria in mind, but all the small

---

the greatest victory today is for us to eliminate terrorism and terrorist thought'), SANA, 6 October 2013, www.sana.sy/?p=2811; 'Hadith Dimashq – faysal miqdad – naib wazir al-kharijiyya al-suri – 30-11-2013' ('Damascus Conversations – Faysal Miqdad – Syrian Vice Minister of the Ministry of Foreign Affairs'), Al Mayadeen Programs (YouTube), 1 December 2013, www.youtube.com/watch?v=LiOvyYBHbh0; 'Al-rais al-assad li qanat khabar al-iraniyya'; 'Muqabalat al-sayyid al-rais bashar al-assad ma' qanat RT al-rusiya 16.03.2023, al-haya al-'ama lil itha'a wal tilfizyun' ('The Interview of His Excellency President Bashar al-Assad with Russian RT Channel 16.03.2023'), (YouTube), 18 March 2023, www.youtube.com/watch?v=V4DvSXdZA84.

[193] 'Liqa d. Faysal miqdad wazir al-kharijiyya wal mughtaribin dhimn barnamaj nuwuyzmaykar' ('Meeting with Dr Faysal al-Miqdad, Vice Minister of the Ministry of Foreign Affairs and Expatriates in the NewsMaker Programme'), BTV (YouTube), 23 May 2024, www.youtube.com/watch?v=y7-g7wzAm34&t=474s.

[194] 'Sha'ban: ma yusama "al-tahaluf al-duwali" lam yakun hadafuh mukafahat al-irhab bal taqdim al-da'm lil majmu'at al-irhabiyya' ('Sha'ban: what is called the "International Coalition" is not aimed at counter-terrorism but to provide aim to terrorist groups'), SANA, 25 November 2017, www.sana.sy/?p=665988; 'Al-Ja'fari: ja'ja'at al-gharb fi majlis al-amn satanhasir ma' hazaim al-irhabiyyin fi suriya' ('Al-Ja'fari: the empty talk of the West in the Security Council will recede with the defeats of the terrorists in Syria'), SANA, 22 March 2018, www.sana.sy/?p=729683.

[195] 'Al-rais al-assad li sahifat tishrin: aham shay fi harb tishrin huwa intisar al-irada wal 'aql al-arabi 'ala al-khawf wal awham'.

countries of the world – whenever it is stronger, and China continues to rise, we feel a greater sense of security'.[196] This is because both Russia and the PRC, which make up 'a pole that believes in justice, sovereignty, and an international relations of parity and equality', have empowered Syria to survive US aggression.[197] This, in turn, has allowed Damascus (as a bulwark and lightening rod) to sap Washington's attention, pulling it away from the theatres of utmost importance to Moscow and Beijing, and thus confirming the Syrian leadership's celebration of their country as a critical force behind the transition to a post-hegemonic 'new world' and, by extension, a post-American regional order.[198]

There is therefore a dialectical dynamic that emerges from the multi-layered arenas of resistance – domestic, regional, and global – that are, eschatologically, contributing to the termination of US power and its replacement with a superior multipolar order. Enduring and waiting for these developments to fully come to fruition is what has guided Syrian foreign policy under the Assad regime. As Sha'ban wrote in an editorial for *al-Mayadeen* entitled 'Farewell to the International Family':

> The era of the colonial Western community and imperial hegemony, which calls itself the 'international family' or 'international community', is waning, and the dawn of a wholly different international family from the east has shone, much like the sun which always dawns from the east, and we live in a period of conflict and confrontation between two camps, two moralities, and different systems of political principles, but the future is certainly to those who truly believe in the freedom of man, and the dignity and equality between all humans, away from the hegemony of the West, and its wars, terrorism, and occupation.[199]

---

[196] 'Al-rais al-assad li qanat rusiya al-yaum: hulm ad-duwal al-gharbiyya wa ba' aduwal al-iqlimiyya bitaqsim suriya la yumkin an yaqbal bihi al-suriyyun – vidyu' ('President al-Assad to the Russian Today Channel: the dream of the Western states and some regional states to dismember Syria will never be accepted by Syrians – videos'), SANA, 14 December 2016, www.sana.sy/?p=480208; 'Safir al-sin bidimashq'.

[197] 'Muqabalat al-sayyid al-rais bashar al-assad ma' tilvizyun al-sin al-markazi'.

[198] 'Marhalat al-muntasirin' ('The phase of the victors'), SANA, 19 July 2014, www.sana.sy/?p=24538; 'Al-rais al-assad fi muqabalah ma' mahatat finiks al-siniyya: turkiyya wal su'udiyya wa qatar yushakilun al-khalfiyya al-da'ima litandim 'da'ish' al-irhabi ... tanbaghi isti'adat al-tawazun fi al-'alam wa tashih al-inhitat al-aklaqi alathi ya'tari al-siyasat al-gharbiyya' ('President al-Assad in an interview with Chinese Phoenix Channel: Türkiye and Saudi Arabia and Qatar constitute the support base for the terrorist ISIS ... The global balance of power must be restored and a course correction to the moral degradation of Western policies'), SANA, 22 November 2015, www.sana.sy/?p=300555; 'Al-doktora sha'ban: suriyya bisumudiha wa intisariha qadamat anamuthajan lil 'alam bina iradat al-shu'ub la tuqhar'.

[199] Buthayna Sha'ban, 'Wada'an lil usra al-duwaliyya' ('Farewell to the international family'), Al-Mayadeen, 24 January 2022, https://short-link.me/14jDF.

China in the Syrian Worldview

Assadist Syrian foreign policy elites have generally espoused a positive view of the PRC, which was consistently depicted as a 'friend-state' (*dawla sadiqa*), if not an outright ally, the term used to describe Russia and Iran.[200] This representation is partially predicated on the recognition that both states are ruled by Leninist parties adopting similar socialist frameworks and anti-imperialist discourses.[201] More significant, however, is the shared sense of victimisation by the US due to their nodal function as strongholds of anti-American resistance: Syria for its role as a lynchpin of the resistance in West Asia, and the PRC as an ascendant challenger to American hegemony in East Asia and beyond. The evidence of American perfidy is, according to the narrative, extensive, beginning with regime change plots. Al-Assad identified the origin of the unrest that was wrecking Syria at present, and had wrecked the PRC many decades before (a likely allusion to the Tiananmen student-led demonstrations), as being one and the same: Western interference.[202] In tandem, the militancy in the XUAR was not viewed as purely a domestic problem for the PRC, but affected Syria in the form of transnational militants.[203] On an altogether different level, Assadist Syrian high-ranking officials such as (the late) Foreign Minister Walid al-Muʿalim, against the backdrop of an intensifying Sino-American trade war in the late 2010s, argued that the PRC and Syria were both subject to 'economic terrorism' (*irhāb iqtisādī*) in the form

---

[200] 'Al-rais al-assad fi muqabala ma' sahifat kathmiri al-yunaniyya: suriya tuharib al-irhabiyyin alathina hum jaysh al-nidham al-turki wal amriki wal su'udi – vidyu' ('President al-Assad in an interview with the Greek Kathmiri Newspaper: Syria is fighting the terrorists who are the army of the Turkish, American, and Saudi regime – video'), SANA, 10 May 2018, www.sana.sy/?p=751436; 'Al-rais al-assad li qanat "finiks" al-siniyya: ay quwat ajnabiyya tadkhul suriya dun da'watina aw ithnina hiya quwat ghaziya – vidyu' ('President al-Assad to the Chinese "Phoenix" Channel: Any foreign forces that enter Syria without our invitation or our permission are invading forces – video'), SANA, 11 March 2017, www.sana.sy/?p=520408; 'Vidyu muqabalat al-rais al-asad ma' finiks al-siniyya' ('Video of President al-Assad's interview with Chinese Phoenix'), Syrian Presidency (YouTube), 16 December 2019, www.youtube.com/watch?v=QkN7HWIsfF8.

[201] 'Al-muhandis al-hilal yabhath fi bikin al-ʿilaqat ma' al-hizb al-shuyu'i al-sini wa subul ta'ziziha' ('The engineer al-Hilal discusses in Beijing relations with the Communist Party and how to strengthen them'), SANA, 19 November 2019, www.sana.sy/?p=1057326; 'Muqabalat al-sayyid al-rais bashar al-assad ma' tilvizyun al-sin al-markazi'.

[202] 'Al-rais al-assad li qanat "finiks" al-siniyya: ay quwat ajnabiyya tadkhul suriya dun da'watina aw ithnina hiya quwat ghaziya – vidyu'.

[203] 'Muqabalat al-rais al-asad ma' finiks al-siniyya' ('President al-Assad's interview with Chinese Phoenix'), Syrian Presidency (YouTube), 16 September 2018, www.youtube.com/watch?v=Qe64wd1F7TY.

of unjust sanctions (most notably the Caesar Syrian Civilian Protection Act) and the monopolisation of key technologies.[204]

Although shared victimisation sets the tone, the discourse on the PRC is refracted primarily through appreciation for the *tangible* actions it was perceived to have undertaken in support of Syria throughout the 2010s. Considerable stress is placed, for instance, on how Western diplomatic double standards and abuses of international law within the halls of the United Nations were decisively countered by Russia and the PRC with sixteen and ten vetoes, respectively, in total in 2011–2020.[205] These stances, al-Assad claimed on Phoenix TV, were driven not by any personal commitment to his person by the Chinese leadership but by their genuine belief in the principles of sovereignty and non-interference.[206] This points to the normative characterisation of PRC diplomacy in Assadist Syrian foreign policy elite discourse. In contrast to the morally depraved and colonially minded US (or more broadly, 'the West'),[207] the PRC is envisioned as an anti-imperial power that fosters peace, civilisational dialogue, and win-win outcomes. Its mediation efforts in bringing about the Saudi–Iranian détente, with its de-escalatory consequences on the regional order, were assessed in similar terms.[208]

Other Chinese contributions, of a military or economic nature, have a more complicated place in the discourse. Unlike Russia or the Islamic Republic, the PRC has neither had a record of military intervention in Syria nor an expectation of it in the discourse (whether at the national or regional scales), a situation which may explain its qualified designation as a friend-state rather than an outright ally. The (then) Syrian

---

[204] 'Naib al-rais al-sini yuakid lil mu'alim istimrar taqdim bikin al-da'm li suriya fi 'ilaqatiha al-thunaiyya wal mahafil ad-duwaliyya wal mundhamat muta'adidat al-atraf' ('The Chinese vice president confirms to al-Mu'alim the continuation of Beijing's provision of support to Syria in their bilateral relations and within international fora and multilateral organizations'), SANA, 17 June 2019, www.sana.sy/?p=963310.

[205] 'Al-Ja'fari: duwal badat turaji' mawqifaha min suriya wa tas'a li i'adat fath qanawat al-itisal' ('Al-Ja'fari: some countries have started to review their positions regarding Syria and to Re-open channels of communication'), SANA, 16 July 2014, www.sana.sy/?p=23128.

[206] 'Muqabalat al-rais al-asad ma' finiks al-siniyya' ('President al-Assad's interview with Chinese Phoenix'), Syrian Presidency (YouTube), 16 September 2018, www.youtube.com/watch?v=Qe64wd1F7TY.

[207] Though Syrian foreign policy elites use Western and American interchangeably, as al-Assad comments in one of his many interviews, the US is the 'maestro' of the Western orchestra. 'Al-rais al-assad li qanat khabar al-iraniyya'.

[208] 'Muqabalat al-sayyid al-rais bashar al-assad ma' tilvizyun al-sin al-markazi'.
'Al-rais al-assad fi muqabalah ma' mahatat finiks al-siniyya: turkiyya wal su'udiyya wa qatar yushakilun al-khalfiyya al-da'ima litandim 'da'ish' al-irhabi ... tanbaghi isti'adat al-tawazun fi al-'alam wa tashih al-inhitat al-aklaqi alathi ya'tari al-siyasat al-gharbiyya'.

ambassador to China, 'Imad Mustapha, in a televised panel on the pro-Syrian al-Mayadeen TV channel covering the Chinese People's Liberation Army high-profile delegation visit to Damascus in mid August 2016, insisted that it was a routine event in the context of nearly thirty years of regular exchange between the two sides: he saw the PRC's vetoes as being of far greater import to Syria.[209] In a similar vein, al-Assad was consistently circumspect about the extent of military cooperation in the Sino-Syrian relationship, emphasising that it had been limited to intelligence gathering and supporting Russia's counter-terrorism operations in the country.[210]

By comparison, the PRC's economic contributions to Syria were much desired and sought after. Tied closely to a vision of Chinese power – as an economic behemoth – the discourse aspirationally viewed the PRC as playing a vital role in stabilising and reconstructing war-torn Syria. The BRI was central to this understanding, though 'Syria is not yet on any of the lines' forming the initiative, as al-Assad noted.[211] This inclusion would not just benefit the country alone, but would, as al-Miqdad claimed in a reiteration of the themes of common victimhood and mutual support, enable the PRC to break Western economic encirclement of Asia.[212] What is notable in the discussions of Assadist Syrian foreign policy elites is how wide the gap is between the PRC's anticipated (and exaggerated) economic role and the mundane (and limited) reality of its actual economic presence on the ground: impediments to investment and trade caused by the security situation, lack of market reciprocity, visa issuance difficulties for businessmen, and the absence of financial channels circumventing Western-imposed

---

[209] 'Al-sin min al-sira' ma' amrika illa al-ta'awun al-'askari ma' suriya' ('China from the rivalry with America to the military cooperation with Syria'), Al-Mayadeen, 5 October 2016, https://short-link.me/14jDR.

[210] 'Muqabalat al-rais al-asad ma' finiks al-siniyya' ('President al-Assad's interview with Chinese Phoenix'), Syrian Presidency (YouTube), 16 September 2018, www.youtube.com/watch?v=Qe64wd1F7TY; 'Al-rais al-assad li qanat khabar al-iraniyya: tasrihat al-masulin al-gharbiyyin al-ijabiyya wal salibiyya la yumkin akhthha 'ala mahmal al-jid li 'adam al-thiqa bihim ... al-juhud al-suriyya al-rusiyya al-iraniyya al-'iraqiyya yajib an yuktab laha al-najah fi mukafahat al-irhab wa illa fanahnu amam tadmir mantiqa bi akmaliha'.

[211] 'Vidyu muqabalat al-rais al-asad ma' finiks al-siniyya' ('Video of President al-Assad with Chinese Phoenix'), Syrian Presidency (YouTube), 16 December 2019, www.youtube.com/watch?v=QkN7HWIsfF8.

[212] 'Al-multaqa al-suri al-sini yurakiz 'ala ta'ziz al-'ilaqat al-iqtisadiyya ... al-miqdad: 'ilaqatuna al-tijariyya la hudada laha-vidyu' ('The Syrian–Chinese gathering focuses on strengthening economic relations ... al-Miqdad: our commercial relations have no boundaries – video'), SANA, 6 December 2016, www.sana.sy/?p=671751.

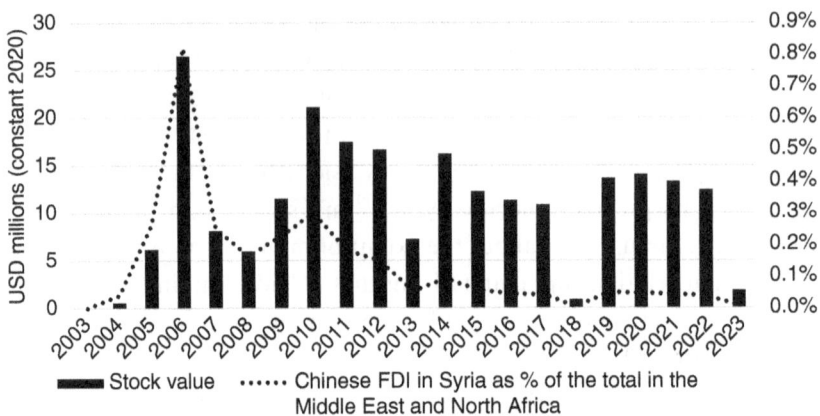

Figure 10 Chinese investment in Syria.

Source: Compiled by the authors using data from the Chinese Ministry of Commerce, China National Bureau of Statistics, and the State Administration of Foreign Exchange.

sanctions are constantly brought up by the highest echelons of the Syrian leaderships.[213]

There are, in fact, signs that the previous prevailing vision of Chinese economic promise moderated in the final years of the regime: in an interview from 2023, al-Assad admitted that the PRC's economic activity was far below what was expected, but he believed that this was due to Syria's insecure domestic circumstances.[214] As Figures 10–12 illustrate, Sino-Syrian economic relations did not recover in the 2010s and early 2020s, suggesting that the PRC's role as an economic saviour, though often spoken about within and outside Syria, remained very much out of reach.[215]

Whatever might be the exact nature of the PRC's contributions to Syria, it was its image as a great power on the verge of replacing the US and reconstituting the international order along more equitable lines that was most significant in this discourse. In the eyes of the Assadist Syrian foreign policy elites, the PRC's aggregation of power could only be a net benefit to

---

[213] 'Sha'ban: sumud suriyya bimusa'adat hulafaiha asasa hilfan qawiyyan fi wajh al-haymana wal irhab' ('Sha'ban: Syria's perseverance with the help of its allies has established a strong alliance in the face of hegemony and terrorism'), SANA, 26 November 2017, www.sana.sy/?p=666399; 'Vidyu muqabalat al-rais al-asad ma' finiks al-siniyya', Syrian Presidency (YouTube), 16 December 2019, www.youtube.com/watch?v=QkN7HWIsfF8.

[214] 'Muqabalat al-sayyid al-rais bashar al-assad ma' tilvizyun al-sin al-markazi'.

[215] Andrea Ghiselli and Mohammed Alsudairi, 'Exploiting China's Rise: Syria's Strategic Narrative and China's Participation in Middle Eastern Politics', *Global Policy* 14 (2023): 19–35.

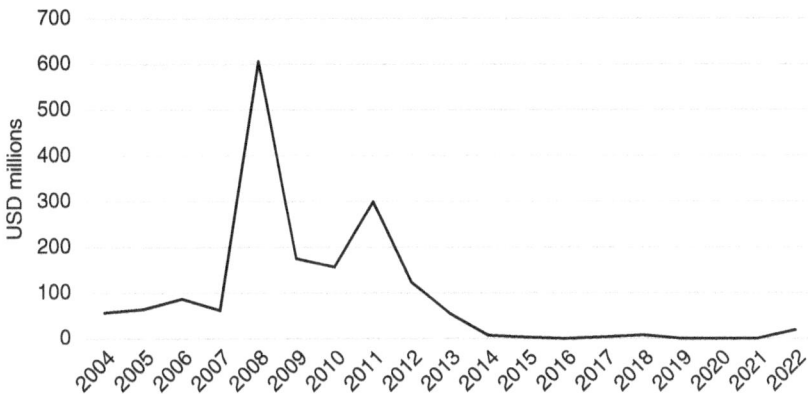

Figure 11 Value of contracts signed by Chinese engineering and construction companies in Syria.

Source: Compiled by the authors using data from the National Bureau of Statistics of China.

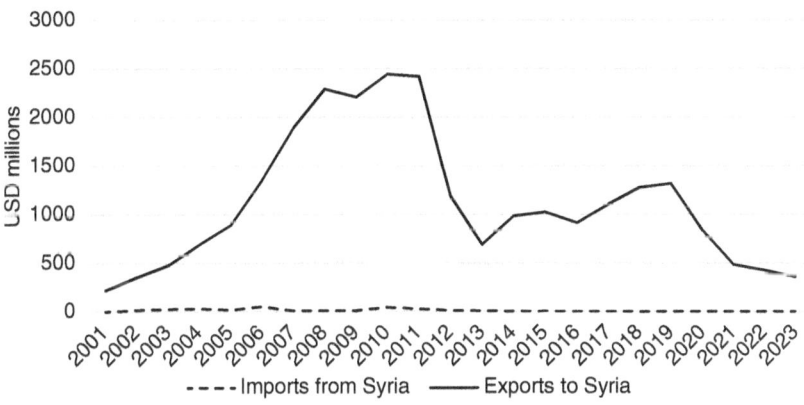

Figure 12 China's trade relations with Syria.

Source: Compiled by the authors using data from the International Trade Centre.

their country, offering Syria the prospect of a post-American geopolitical environment. Sha'ban thus proclaimed that 'the future lies with those new alliances in East Asia, China, and Iran', explaining in turn the country's earnest embrace of an 'eastward policy' (*siyasat al-itijah sharqan*).[216] Likewise, al-Assad, who was in the habit of boasting how his son Karim was studying Mandarin to many Chinese media-linked journalists, connected this

---

[216] 'Sha'ban: mubadarat "al-hizam wal tariq" badil lil haymana al-gharbiyya' ('Sha'ban: The "Belt and Road" Initiative is an alternative to Western hegemony'), SANA, 26 April 2019, http://sana.sy/?p=937433.

choice with the PRC's coming dominance on the global stage.[217] The BRI was viewed as an important instrument in accelerating Chinese ascendancy and multipolarisation: al-Assad called the initiative a harbinger of a re-distributary shift from (Western) zero-sum to (non-Western) cooperative modes of global politics, while Sha'ban described it as a 'fundamental solution' (*hal jathrī*) to the problems of mankind.[218]

On the Syrian Vision

In this section we probed how Assadist Syrian foreign policy elites viewed the regional order and the PRC's role in that. We find that they articulated a campist vision of the Middle East defined primarily by one's relationality towards American imperial hegemony. They see this division (and the influence exerted by the US) as underpinning not only the lack of regional integration (given the polarisation of local state actors along pro- and anti-US lines) but also the instability within Syria itself. Connected to this, they saw the regime's principled safeguarding of the country's sovereignty and national interests – antithetical to US ambitions in the region – as the primary reason behind the tribulations Syria had experienced. At the same time, they held to an optimistic and even messianic reading of the future: their country and its regional allies were posed to ultimately triumph and free the Middle East from the shackles of US control. This assessment stemmed not only from their very survival over the course of a decade but also from what they perceived as an ongoing and irreversible redistribution of global power that reinforced region-wide resistance.

Within this framework, the PRC was understood to play an important role, facilitating broader multipolarisation and extending vital aid to Syria. Beyond instances of diplomatic support, however, Sino-Syrian relations – especially in the military and economic domains – remained limited, though there was much more hope placed on the latter than the former. Taking all this into consideration, it is clear that the PRC was conceived as one (important) variable among many that contributed to the birth of a post-American regional order, though how and when this might

---

[217] 'Al-rais al-assad fi muqabalah ma' mahatat finiks al-siniyya: turkiyya wal su'udiyya wa qatar yushakilun al-khalfiyya al-da'ima litandim "da'ish" al-irhabi ... tanbaghi isti'adat al-tawazun fi al-'alam wa tashih al-inhitat al-aklaqi alathi ya'tari al-siyasat al-gharbiyya'.

[218] 'Vidyu muqabalat al-rais al-asad ma' finiks al-siniyya' ('Video of President al-Assad with Chinese Phoenix'), Syrian Presidency (YouTube), 16 December 2019, www.youtube.com/watch?v=QkN7HWIsfF8; 'Sha'ban: mubadarat "al-hizam wal tariq" badil lil haymana al-gharbiyya'.

happen was left unsaid. While there was an abiding belief that the Middle East was undergoing positive change and would continue to do so over the short and medium terms, Syria had no option but to 'wait' (or endure and resist) until US power was sufficiently degraded and constrained. Notably, there was no discernible anticipation among Assadist Syrian foreign policy elites of any major change in Chinese foreign policy. In addition, they did not seem to expect that the PRC would embed itself in the regional security architecture or take on a role akin to that of the US.

Conclusion

The picture emerging from the previous sections is a complex and nuanced one. On the one hand, all the examined clusters of foreign policy elites ascribe growing importance to Sino-Middle Eastern relations. They treat these relationships, in the bilateral and multilateral scales, as drivers – now and into the future – behind a much desired regional re-ordering, as well as a broader (and perhaps inevitable) trend towards global multipolarisation. On the other hand, they all display variations in their specific assessments about the future of the Middle East, which, they all agree, is currently in a state of interregnum and transition.

Chinese and Assadist Syrian foreign policy elites, for instance, espoused a similar teleological narrative in which the region, long plagued by US subversion, was believed to be headed towards a post-American future due to various multi-scalar dynamics (specifically, intra-regional integration and the aggregation of power by opponents of the US). A passive 'waiting' for this endpoint to materialise is what is essentially called for by these elites. This approach resonates with the prevailing perspective voiced by the PRC leadership of 'great changes unseen in a century' ('bǎinián wèi yǒu zhī dà biànjú') in which they view the country's rejuvenation as being driven by, and in turn propelling, a positive yet turbulent change in the global order.[219] Although some in the PRC have started to talk about the necessity of embracing a more assertive approach towards the region in tandem with these shifts, this is far from being a mainstream position given the risks associated with such a policy change.

The Saudi foreign policy elites, by contrast, have rejected the passivity of their counterparts, seeing ample room (and an existential necessity) for a

---

[219] He Cheng, 'Quánmiàn rènshí hé lǐjiě "bǎinián wèi yǒu zhī dà biànjú"' ('Comprehensively recognise and understand "changes unforeseen in a century"'), *Renminwang*, 3 January 2020, http://theory.people.com.cn/n1/2020/0103/c40531-31533088.html.

more activist approach that could re-shape the regional order and contain the damage unleashed by problematic regional actors such as Iran.[220] While this perspective in Saudi foreign policy thinking could be interpreted as reflecting Riyadh's ongoing crisis of trust with Washington, those involved in these debates are unequivocal in their desire and support for a continued security connection with the US: a post-American Middle East is simply not a palatable scenario to them. That they emphasise a primarily diplomatic and economic toolkit for resolving regional problems is also indicative of the limits of Saudi power projection, at least for the foreseeable future.

Geopolitical cleavages and distinct ideological commitments – that is, which camps these elites fall into – might account for many of these differences, but we also see various combinations of interests and capabilities, as understood by each of these foreign policy elites, as playing a major determining role. The PRC is the most powerful state among the three by far, but it faces many challenges – domestic and in other proximate theatres of importance (the Asia-Pacific) – that make active and systematic investment (in terms of strategic focus and resources) in a faraway arena such as the Middle East difficult to justify in comparison with maintaining a more opportunistic and transactional approach, at least for the time being.[221] Although American pressure is increasingly being felt in domains such as technological cooperation with respect to Sino-Middle Eastern ties, the PRC's core interests, however conceived, remain largely unthreatened by the current status quo in the region. Though it has vast capabilities, its incentives for involvement in the context of the Middle East are, in other words, limited.

Assadist Syria, the weakest among the three, had the greatest interest, or so it would appear, in realising a truly post-American region, yet given its own devastation over the course of the 2010s, it hardly had the capacity to contest the presence of American troops on its own soil (stationed there even well after the collapse of the regime), let alone to influence events beyond its borders.[222] As we see it, the confidence of Chinese and Assadist

---

[220] Containment and rollback were intentionally used to highlight the inadvertent parallels between contemporary Saudi policy vis-à-vis the Islamic Republic in the 2010s with that of the US towards the communist bloc in the 1950s in so far as their basic impulses, and the contradictions they faced, were concerned; see László Borhi, 'Rollback, Liberation, Containment, or Inaction? US Policy and Eastern Europe in the 1950s', *Journal of Cold War Studies* 1, no. 3 (1999): 67–110.

[221] Our take accords with the concentric conceptualisation of the PRC's national security as discussed in Andrew James and Andrew Scobell, *China's Search for Security* (Columbia University Press, 2012).

[222] There are, of course, various opinions in the US about this military presence in Syria; see Charles Lister, 'America Is Planning to Withdraw from Syria – and Create a Disaster', *Foreign Affairs*, 24 January 2024, https://foreignpolicy.com/2024/01/24/

Syrian foreign policy elite in the future belied the fact that neither the PRC or Assadist Syria could or should exercise, albeit for different reasons, a more direct role in regional affairs. Saudi Arabia, by comparison, had significant stakes in shaping the regional landscape (specifically, protecting its ongoing domestic development project from negative externalities), as well as the capabilities to do so (though perhaps reaching the limits of its military capacities, as the intervention in Yemen showed), placing it equidistant between the other two.[223]

One notable narrational thread that must be stressed is that none of the foreign policy elites examined spoke of the PRC as a military actor embedded, now or in the future, within the regional security architecture. Instead, almost all had opted to focus on its economic prowess and the influence that derives, or should derive, from that source. While this is very much in line with what one would expect from Chinese foreign policy elites, the absence of a substantive discussion of a PRC military role in the Saudi and Assadist Syrian cases is interesting given the zeitgeist surrounding a post-American region. It might reflect an instance where such elites, due to their decades-long exposure to Chinese diplomacy-speak, have internalised expectations about the range and limitations of what is possible in terms of PRC behaviour. This is discernible in how even in the starkly campist world vision of the Assadist leadership, the PRC as an allied military actor – in Syria or the region more broadly – is somewhat missing. There could be something similar at play among Saudi foreign policy elites, though this would be operating in conjunction with their well-ingrained pro-American orientation when it comes to the country's national security. Far more confidence, outstripping even that of their Chinese counterparts, is placed by Saudi and Assadist Syrian foreign policy elites in the PRC's economic (and, by extension, diplomatic) influence in so far as it is seen to potentially advance their domestic and regional agendas.[224] This is an attitude likely shared by other elites in the region.

---

america-is-planning-to-withdraw-from-syria-and-create-a-disaster/; Adam Weinstein and Steven Simon, 'Troops in Peril: The Risks of Keeping U.S. Troops in Iraq and Syria', Quincy Institute for Responsible Statecraft, 15 April 2024, https://quincyinst.org/research/troops-in-peril-the-risks-of-keeping-u-s-troops-in-iraq-and-syria/.

[223] This assertion does not imply that it will necessarily succeed, but rather that at least for the 2010s Saudi Arabia has radically transformed its diplomatic, military, and economic approaches to the Middle East in a more interventionist and activist direction. It is a state that has the economic wealth and political capital to aspire to change the region in its image.

[224] Such developments are playing out with respect to techno-scientific cooperation, see Mohammed Al-Sudairi, Steven Jiawei Hai, and Kameal Alahmad, 'How Saudi Arabia Bent China to Its Technoscientific Ambitions', Carnegie Endowment, 1 August 2023,

Generalising the findings from the case studies requires great care. This is especially so when their number is small relative to the much larger and more diverse group of state (and sub-state) actors found in the Middle East. In addition, one of them had been recently overthrown, with a new regime (led by HTS) established in its place. That said, we believe that the study of Saudi and Assadist Syrian narratives can still provide us with important insights into the broad dynamics of Sino-Middle Eastern relations as we look at where other countries in the region are located along the two key spectrums mentioned in the introduction of this Element: proximity to/distance from the US; and those countries' internal capabilities.

In essence, we believe that there are two clusters of actors in the region. The first is composed of a diverse set of countries which constitute what we call the 'irrelevant extremes'. These are made up of powerful and highly capable actors such as Israel and Iran that strongly support the persistence (and even expansion) of the US-dominated regional order or its radical overthrow, respectively, as well as countries that possess little in the way of diplomatic, economic, and military clout, such as Lebanon, Tunisia, Libya, and Sudan. Assadist Syria was representative of this 'double' extremism. We argue that such actors are unlikely to determine the future of Sino-Middle Eastern relations due to their lack of critical mass, both individually and collectively – either because their preferences for the regional order are too unpalatable and radical (both for the wider Middle East and the PRC) or because they are unable to make them felt.[225] The second group, instead, is made up of countries we dub the 'consequential swing states'. These include actors such as Saudi Arabia and Türkiye which are functionally high-value hedgers – that is, secondary states – whose capabilities afford them the potential to reshape the regional order and tip the scales in the context of great power rivalry.[226] Such states might signal strong (even extreme) alignment with one camp (i.e., the US) and desire

---

https://carnegieendowment.org/research/2023/08/how-saudi-arabia-bent-china-to-its-technoscientific-ambitions?lang=en.

[225] There is also the question of how their positionalities vis-à-vis the US impact their relations with the PRC. Israel's alliance with the US has had a constraining effect on its technological, military, and even economic relationship with the PRC over the past two decades. In a different way, the US-imposed sanctions regime on the Islamic Republic has limited the extent of its substantive cooperation with the PRC; see Shira Efron, Howard J. Shatz, Arthur Chan, Emily Haskel, Lyle J. Morris, and Andrew Scobell, *The Evolving Israel-China Relationship* (Rand Corporation, 2019); Jacopo Scita, 'China-Iran Relations through the Prism of Sanctions', *Asian Affairs* 53, no. 1 (2022): 87–105.

[226] Luis Simón and Fabio Figiaconi. 'Better Safe Than Sorry: Why Great Powers Accommodate High-Value Hedgers', *Review of International Studies* (2024): 1–19.

'formalised' admission through defensive treaties and arrangements but are simultaneously hedging if circumstances change.

Considering the findings from the various sections through the lens of the framework that we outlined in the Introduction, it appears that the first of the three scenarios regarding the future of Sino-Middle East relations is the most likely for the late 2020s and early 2030s: a continued emphasis on interdependent economic ties, couched in developmental terms, with no major security entanglement for the PRC whatsoever. When taking the debates within Beijing into account, there is little appetite for a much larger role within the Middle East in which most Chinese core interests remain well protected. Neither is there a *Pax Sinica* in the minds of regional elites – whether they hail from the irrelevant extremes or the consequential swing states. All this suggests that the current status quo, in terms of the PRC's regional order as a purely economic actor, is acceptable to the majority of the key regional stakeholders and will likely endure for some time to come. After all, if elites on both sides have no interest in exploring an option (of, say, Chinese involvement in the Middle East's security architecture), the likelihood of its occurrence, so long as things hold, is slim.

These findings are an important corrective to an all too common narrative that depicts the PRC in constant ascendancy in the Middle East, displacing US influence whenever and wherever possible as part of its global strategy of domination.[227] By interrogating the ways in which foreign policy elites in Beijing and (some) Arab capitals interpret regional dynamics, and the implications of Chinese interests and actions there, we have presented a more mundane, yet realistic, picture: the PRC is but one actor among many in the Middle East, operating within existing material constraints and conservative ideational perceptions (both locally and in Beijing) of how it might exercise its great power status there.[228] While American influence might be waning, one cannot but take notice of how – implicitly or explicitly, and with different degrees of satisfaction or dissatisfaction – Chinese

---

[227] It aligns moreover – albeit while coming from a different angle – with the findings of scholars and experts about the circumscribed role of the PRC in the Middle East; see, for example, Tim Niblock, 'China and the Middle East: A Global Strategy Where the Middle East Has a Significant but Limited Place', *Asian Journal of Middle Eastern and Islamic Studies* 14, no. 4 (2020): 481–504; Andrew Scobell, 'What China Wants in the Middle East', United States Institute of Peace, 1 November 2023; Jonathan Fulton, 'China Doesn't Have as Much Leverage in the Middle East as One Thinks – at Least When It Comes to Iran', Atlantic Council, 1 February 2024; Sun Yun, 'China Wants to Weaken, not Replace, the U.S. in the Middle East', *Foreign Affairs*, 29 February 2024; 'Congressional Testimony by Jon B. Alterman', CSIS, 19 April 2024.

[228] We agree with the findings of Dale Aluf, 'Mirage of Coercion: The Real Sources of China's Influence in the Middle East and North Africa', *Survival* 66, no. 5 (2024): 159–182.

and regional elites do not see American power being surpassed any time soon. If anything, some seek to maintain and shore it up.

Our centring of local perspectives reveals a very different vision (or set of visions) about the regional order and the PRC's place within it, and one that we believe more closely approximates the realities of the present moment and its future trajectory. These visions are durable, furthermore, offering mental roadmaps on how these states 'see' and 'interact' with the world. The outbreak of a new round of violence between Israel and Hamas (and, by extension, the wider so-called axis of resistance) since October 2023 – barely outside our temporal cut-off – or the overthrow of the Assadist regime has not changed the basic contours of how Chinese or Saudi foreign policy elites assess things. If anything, the events appear to have confirmed their well-ingrained biases and interpretations of regional dynamics, both in the PRC and within the Middle East.[229] In the case of Syria, the new HTS-led regime inherited the same limitations in capabilities as the former regime, though its positionality (especially vis-à-vis the US) is in flux. It remains to be seen how things will evolve with the PRC given pending issues like that of the Uyghur militant fighters, but there is, we believe, a substantive pathway for Sino-Syrian economic relations to grow if Chinese diplomatic (and national) priorities are satisfied and Western sanctions are fully lifted. In that sense, the new Syria has a chance to move, with respect to its ties with the PRC, in a direction similar to that found elsewhere in the region, becoming less extreme perhaps, but no less irrelevant.

We emphasise that our predictions for Sino-Middle Eastern relations are not static, and many possible developments or variables (conceived as 'black swans' or 'grey rhinos') could erode or overturn the narrational structures that underpin them. We identify at least three interconnected factors that could augur such a change in how the future of Sino-Middle Eastern relations might unfold: a major shift in the character of Sino-American competition; the ongoing transformation of the PRC economy; and domestic developments among and within local state actors themselves.

As to the first factor, the debates on the US in Beijing, and equivalent ones on the PRC in Washington, have clearly become more difficult and intense over the past decade. Across multiple issues, ranging from trade volumes, capital flows, to technological innovation, there is a growing sense of zero-sum rivalry and global-level encirclement and containment on both

---

[229] Fardella and Ghiselli, *Power Shifts?*; Shiyao Wu, 'Zhōngdōng guójiā "xiàng dōng kàn" jí qí duì huá zhèngcè xuǎnzé' ('The Middle East Countries' "Look East" Strategy and Their Strategic Choice Toward China'), *Foreign Affairs Review* 3 (2024): 54–79.

sides, and one that is perceived as unfolding in various theatres, including the Middle East. If Sino-American relations undergo another severe downturn with no possible resolution in sight or – and this is perhaps more unrealistic given our temporal horizon of a decade – if US decline vis-à-vis China becomes far more obvious in all key areas of national power, then the PRC – which has so far been cautious in its responses – might opt to pursue an interventionist foreign policy in the region aimed at challenging US efforts to restrict its techno-economic interests there.[230] To a minor extent, a renewed American push to isolate or pursue regime change in Iran could also trigger a Chinese response. Not only would that undermine China's regional diplomatic interests and energy supplies, but it would also have negative repercussions for Russia. Naturally, the eruption of military hostilities over Taiwan would have enormous ramifications as well, with significant political, economic, and social reverberations. The Chinese reaction to any of these events would entail involvement in the domestic politics of local state actors, as well as regional disputes, and would therefore likely affect the perception of the PRC in those places. Our expectation, however, is that only an extreme situation, and one that directly harms national core interests, would lead to such a break in Chinese foreign policy, which will (likely) still be impacted by a hierarchy of priorities that ultimately treat the Middle East as a third- or fourth-tier arena of strategic importance. At the time of writing, Beijing's relative 'absence' with respect to the Israeli–Iranian War, despite widespread claims about the twenty-five-year strategic partnership between China and Iran (and its presumed military implications), seems to substantiate our appraisal.

Turning to the PRC economy, it is worth recalling that the Chinese leadership has been attempting structural reform for well over a decade now.[231] Its aim in doing so is to unleash technology-focused 'new quality productive forces' ('xīnzhí shēngchǎnlì'), moving the economy away from a conventional debt-fuelled model of growth and achieving some degree of technological 'self-reliance' ('zìlì gēngshēng'). At the same time, PRC

---

[230] For some instances of these battlefronts, see John Calabrese, 'The Huawei Wars and the 5G Revolution in the Gulf', The Middle East Institute, 30 July 2019; Cathrin Schaer, 'US-China "Tech War": AI Sparks First Battle in Middle East', Deutsche Welle, 10 February 2023, www.dw.com/en/us-china-tech-war-ai-sparks-first-battle-in-middle-east/a-66968886; Chloe Cornish and Kaye Wiggins, 'Abu Dhabi AI Group G42 Sells Its China Stakes to Appease US', The Financial Times, 10 February 2024, www.ft.com/content/82473ec4-fa7a-43f2-897c-ceb9b10ffd7a.

[231] For a good overview of the Chinese leadership's efforts and challenges in the economic sphere, see Max J. Zenglein and Jacob Gunter, The Party Knows Best: Aligning Economic Actors with China's Strategic Goals (MERICS, October 2023).

policymakers have put efforts into making the country's economy more energy efficient. These are all developments that many local state actors in the Middle East are particularly attentive to. Hydrocarbon-producing countries, such as Saudi Arabia, depend on the revenues from the Chinese market to finance their own economic reforms and preserve domestic stability. Concurrently, they increasingly see Chinese capital, technology, and even the mobilities of Chinese consumers as vital for their industrialisation and post-rentierist projects. For less capable (and resource-poor) states, the importance attributed to Chinese capital is even greater. As such, whether the Chinese economy will stagnate and, to a minor extent, whether it will become less energy hungry due to its ongoing energy transition could have repercussions on the region. After all, the PRC's most significant strength in the eyes of Middle Eastern foreign policy elites is its economy.[232] We should not discount, moreover, how changes in regional economies might lead to the emergence of new and unanticipated synergies, as well as competitive pressures, within Sino-Middle Eastern ties (the two decades-long gridlock over negotiating a GCC–China free trade agreement, centred primarily on the petrochemical sector, is a demonstrative example of this).[233] Such changes could influence the material underpinnings of these ties and lead regional and Chinese elites to re-evaluate the strategic importance (or prioritisation) of their connections. One should not over-exaggerate this, however. There are developmental (hierarchical) disparities between China and the Middle East that are likely to ensure continued compatibility. The Sino-American trade war, which in our estimation is an expression of a long-term structural confrontation between these two great powers, might temper this potential problem further as Beijing prioritises expanding trade with (and industrial outsourcing in) the Global South (including the Middle East) in order to achieve some limited de-coupling from the US.

Last, but not least, Sino-Middle Eastern relations today are sustained by policy and perceptional convergence over key issues such as regime stability and survival, especially in the post-Arab Spring era. This is because

---

[232] While disappointment might have been long felt in the case of Assadist Syria, it could also manifest within Sino-Saudi relations (and elsewhere) as they begin to reach their structural limitations; see Mohammed Turki Al-Sudairi, 'An Overview of Sino-Gulf Relations: A "New Era" of Growth and a Future Era of Stagnation?' in Enrico Fardella and Andrea Ghiselli, (eds.), *ChinaMed Report 2019: China's New Role in the Wider Mediterranean Region* (ChinaMed, 2019), 50–57.

[233] One area of energy-centric cooperation is in the GCC supplying computing power for the PRC and other actors; see Abdullah Alzabin, 'PetroCompute: Will A.I.'s Future Run through the Gulf?', Alzabin Substack, 17 December 2024, https://alzabin.substack.com/p/petrocompute-will-ais-future-run.

many regimes, from the Gulf monarchies to the Arab republics, have spent significant energy at keeping Islamist forces at bay while also leaning into economic development as one of the main sources of legitimacy, an approach that comfortably matches the PRC's own foreign policy and domestic preferences.[234] Societies and leaders are not static, however. Mismanagement and failure to deliver might lead to a new round of revolutionary uprisings and even civil wars, an acute risk in North Africa and evident in recent developments there. Continued breakdown in the regional order would likely play a role in changing existing dynamics, either eroding further the importance of the Middle East to the PRC (i.e., confirming deeply ingrained perceptions of disorder and chaos) – the more likely outcome – or perhaps pushing some Chinese foreign policy elites to embrace more interventionist policies. The ongoing Israeli-bid for regional hegemony, possible Iranian nuclearization, and the balancing counter-reactions of Türkiye and Saudi Arabia, could lead us down such a path as well.

These events all exist within the realm of possibility, although, for now, their probable realisation remain relatively low. A deterioration in Sino-American relations under the new Trump administration is possible, but the outbreak of war remains improbable. A slowdown in the Chinese economy is likely, but its collapse is not. The Middle East itself is undergoing a period of profound change, but not necessarily in a way that will end the substantial alignment of interests between Beijing and most regional actors. Hence, future research will surely have to pay attention to these factors as scholars and analysts continue to observe the evolution of the relations between the region and the PRC in an increasingly changing world. For now, however, we judge that the basic pattern of Sino-Middle Eastern relations will continue into the foreseeable future, with a collectively perceived 'ceiling' that constrains the transformation of these ties in a more strategically substantive direction.[235] In the eyes of the foreign policy elites that behold them in Beijing and Arab capitals, this is a wholly acceptable state of affairs, though their counterparts in Washington might think otherwise.

---

[234] Amjed Rasheed, 'The Narrative of the Rise of China and Authoritarianism in the Global South: The Case of Egypt', *The International Spectator* 57, no. 2 (2022): 68–84; Will Cochrane-Dye, 'Arab Media Portrayals of Anti-Uyghur Repression: Chinese Propaganda, Anti-Islamist Anxiety, and Anti-Westernism', *The Middle East Journal* 77, no. 1 (2023): 79–96.

[235] It is worth noting that despite the immense diplomatic opportunities created by the current moment of drawn-out crisis caused by the October 7 attacks in 2024, the PRC has not pursued any fundamentally new policies in the region; see Lina Benabdallah, 'Between Pragmatism and Ideology: Rethinking China-MENA relations in the time of crises', *POMEPS Studies* 54 (February 2025): 20–24.

… Cambridge Elements ⁼

Middle East Politics

David B. Roberts
King's College London

David B. Roberts is a Reader in International Security and Middle East Studies at King's College London. He is also the Head of Professional Education and Enterprise in the King's Institute for Applied Security Studies (KIASS) and leads a twin-track Arabic and English Master of Research (MRes) programme in the School of Security Studies.

Louise Fawcett
University of Oxford

Louise Fawcett is Professor of International Relations and Senior Research Fellow at the Department of Politics and International Relations, and Fellow of St Catherine's College, University of Oxford. She is a co-director of the Oxford Martin School programme, 'Changing Global Order' (https://www.politics.ox.ac.uk/project/oxford-martin-programme-changing-global-order).

Mohammed Abdel-Haq
King's College London

Dr Mohammed Abdel-Haq is a Professor in Banking and the Director of the Centre for Islamic Finance, the Director of the Centre for Opposition Studies and Assistant Vice Chancellor for Postgraduate Development at the University of Bolton. He is also the Principal of Hume Institute for Postgraduate Studies, Lausanne, Switzerland; Affiliate Professor, Kings College London and an Associate at London School of Economics – IDEAS.

About the Series

Elements in Middle East Politics provides a platform for scholars to explore subjects of contemporary resonance in relation to the broader Middle East at a time when this most pivotal of regions faces profound flux. Studies focus on thematic and country focused analyses, as well ideas and approaches that seek to decolonize knowledge and highlight new disciplinary trends.

Cambridge Elements⹀

Middle East Politics

Elements in the Series

What is the Middle East?: The Theory and Practice of Regions
Marc Lynch

Narratives of Sino-Middle Eastern Futures: In the Eye of the Beholder
Mohammed Alsudairi and Andrea Ghiselli

A full series listing is available at: www.cambridge.org/EMEP

Printed by Integrated Books International,
United States of America